Displacement, (De)segregation, and Dispossession

Rebecca Alexander

Displacement, (De)segregation, and Dispossession

Race-class Frontiers in the Transition to High School

The Education Studies Collection

Collection editor

Dr Janise Hurtig

This book is dedicated to the young people, families, teachers, school leaders, and community organizers who entrusted me with their stories, experiences, concerns, and ideas. I am forever grateful for all that you shared.

First published in 2024 by Lived Places Publishing

All rights reserved. No part of this publication may be reproduced, stored in a retrieval system, or transmitted in any form or by any means, electronic, mechanical, photocopying, recording or otherwise, without prior permission in writing from the publisher.

The authors and editors have made every effort to ensure the accuracy of information contained in this publication, but assumes no responsibility for any errors, inaccuracies, inconsistencies and omissions. Likewise, every effort has been made to contact copyright holders. If any copyright material has been reproduced unwittingly and without permission the Publisher will gladly receive information enabling them to rectify any error or omission in subsequent editions.

Copyright © 2024 Lived Places Publishing

British Library Cataloguing in Publication Data
A CIP record for this book is available from the British Library

ISBN: 9781915271068 (pbk)
ISBN: 9781915271082 (ePDF)
ISBN: 9781915271075 (ePUB)

The right of Rebecca Alexander to be identified as the Author of this work has been asserted by them in accordance with the Copyright, Design and Patents Act 1988.

Cover design by Fiachra McCarthy
Book design by Rachel Trolove of Twin Trail Design
Typeset by Newgen Publishing UK

Lived Places Publishing
Long Island
New York 11789

www.livedplacespublishing.com

Abstract

Drawing on two years of fieldwork in "Glenview," a historically Black suburb, and "Westside," the historically white, wealthy community just across the freeway, this book analyzes segregation and gentrification in schools and communities. Situated in California during the 2007–2008 sub-prime crisis, the text follows nine young people from different sides of a race-class neighborhood border as they transition from racially isolated middle schools to a diverse but internally segregated high school. Locating the schools within the broader histories of these communities, the text illuminates how youth and families work to produce, contest, and engage racialized space in and beyond schools.

Keywords

School Segregation, Desegregation, Middle School, High School, Race, Dispossession, Gentrification, Frontier, Community, Family, Tracking.

Contents

Introduction — 1

    Chapter 1 Memo: This school is for the white kids — 31

    Chapter 2 Jaqueline: It's nice but not for us — 51

    Chapter 3 Cam: Because she was taking care of me — 75

    Chapter 4 Amy: The real world — 93

    Chapter 5 Khalil: They played me — 115

    Chapter 6 Talli: You stay with your own kind — 137

    Chapter 7 Rahul: Fuck this school — 157

    Chapter 8 Jonathan: I know everybody — 177

    Chapter 9 Elijah: The sky's not the limit — 191

Conclusions: Education, abolition, segregation, dispossession, decoloniality — 211

Notes — 217

References — 218

Recommended projects, assignments, and discussion questions — 230

Suggested further reading — 233

Index — 241

Introduction

A "high school transition meeting" for students planning to attend Westside High School (Westside) was announced on a Thursday afternoon at Dolores Huerta Middle School (Huerta). News of the meeting had just arrived from the district, although the meeting was to be held later that same day. Student volunteers were sent to the eighth-grade classrooms to tell anyone who would be attending Westside High School to call their parents because there would be a meeting that evening at 6:00 with school officials. At 6:00 p.m., a small handful of families were perched awkwardly on the tiny round plastic seats of the fold-down school lunch tables. The high school officials—eight of them in total, dressed in suits and business casual—fiddled with a slide projector perched in the middle of the cafeteria, shining its trapezoidal light onto the far wall where it was distorted by an outcropping. There were piles of handouts on the stage. Everyone was silent except the youngest children, who fidgeted.

As the first official took the microphone for introductions, it became apparent this was intended to be a meeting for the Westside school district, not just Westside High School, and that all four district high schools would be presenting. Unfortunately, only students thinking of attending Westside High—a school that was not the default school for most Huerta students—were present. No one corrected this error. Instead, the officials proceeded with slide presentations describing the assets of their campuses: robotics classes, a full slate of honors and AP courses, a water polo team, a brand-new theater, touch screen white boards. They described courses most Huerta students would have no access to, even if they attended these schools. Many would be placed in remedial courses, requiring them to attend extra periods of non-college-prep English and math, foregoing all electives. Others, placed in higher tracks, would be shut out because of jobs, long commutes, family responsibilities, and fees. None of the speakers addressed this.

The third speaker was from Elmwood School, the assigned school for most Huerta students. She did not have a PowerPoint, but instead held up a stack of photocopied papers. "I wasn't sure what kind of meeting this was going to be," she said, "so I brought copies of the school rules." She continued, "a lot of students from this district seem to have trouble with the school rules, so I thought it was important to make sure you understand them before you enter our schools." She handed copies to the tables and returned to her seat. Moments like this, in which Huerta students were framed and approached as problems, were part of what made teachers from Huerta very worried about how their students were treated in the transition to high school and at Westside district schools.

Dolores Huerta Middle School

Huerta was a big school surrounded by a chain link fence. Students regularly spelled out messages to the community by poking Dixie cups between the fence links to form large dot-letters. The first day I visited, they had written "stop the violence;" another day they wrote "love your roots." The school was on the east side of an eight-lane freeway, in the heart of Glenview, a working-class community of color in California. A Catholic church stood next door. Between the church and school, a woman sold elotes (corn on the cob) and chicharrones (pork rinds) to passers-by from a pushcart. Parents and children clustered at the bus stops and filled the sidewalks of Creek Road, the busy suburban street in front of the school. On the school side of the fence, students could usually be seen walking or running around the track that surrounded the soccer field. A colorful mural of a giant eagle painted on one of the walls was visible in the distance.

Mr Flores, the principal at Huerta, like many other local organizers, graduated from a nearby university. As a corps member with Teach for America, he was initially assigned to teach in Glenview but resigned to more effectively organize for change in the district after a number of his friends were fired for "political reasons." "I was a very big union rabble rouser," he recalled; "I led a funeral march with the union down the street." The movement got media attention and propelled a change in district leadership. As a school leader at Huerta, Mr Flores had worked to build a positive school climate, reduce teacher turnover, and develop the school as a community center.

Mr Flores felt things were better in the district, but that there was much more work to do: "we have those conversations all the time … we need to make sure that we're using best practices, we need to make sure that we're rigorous." But he also reflected on the broader context of the district: "when you say Glenview, there's usually just a couple [of districts] that are kind of approximately similar." He described asking other school leaders at a statewide gathering: "Who has above 90 percent free and reduced lunch? Who has above 80 percent immigrant population? Who has full inclusion with special education?" He described watching hands steadily drop until only a few leaders, with similar demographics, had their hands raised. Particularly intractable, he argued, were the "intense mandates both from the state, because we are underperforming, but also from the federal courts, because of a special education lawsuit" which was written in a way that made it very difficult to exit oversight.

One of the most frustrating parts of the work was the lack of respect from nearby communities and state entities. "A lot of what adults experience who work in … our district is just regular, um, derision and skepticism and condescension. Never mind the fact," he went on, "that people write movies and books about single teachers who can get results with just one class worth of our kids. Like freedom writers, whoop de whoop, you know, *Dangerous Minds*, whoop de whoop … 'Stand and Deliver, whoop de whoop.' All this bullshit," he kept going, "I mean imagine, it's such a big deal when just one teacher can get results that nobody would care about in Glenview. It's such a big deal that a movie and a book is written about it and it's watched in the ghetto across the nation. Like how many times did I grow up and have to watch Stand and Deliver, like every Latino from [the area's] probably watched Stand and Deliver like eight times, you know!! Like wow, you're really connecting with me."

The sense of caring community, academic rigor, and community-driven pedagogy Mr Flores had sought to create were evident throughout the school. But the struggles of the school and the district were also very clear. At Huerta middle school there were few computers in classrooms. The two computer labs with working desktop computers were poorly maintained, particularly after the technology support staff were sacrificed to budget cuts. One teacher, Mr Jackson, brought in a small inexpensive LCD projector for his classroom purchased with his own money. Many teachers functioned without a projector or borrowed one from Mr Jackson or the principal (when the school projector was working). Were it not for a 21st century grant to extend the school day in an effort to raise test scores[1], Huerta would have had no extracurricular courses or activities at all—no art, music, woodshop, photography, or sports program. They did not have a functioning science lab and students received science instruction only once per week.

The introduction of new facilities or equipment, in and of themselves, would make limited difference at Huerta. Rather, as the budget cuts Huerta and all Glenview schools went through in 2007–2008 and 2008–2009 made clear, it was not the material goods per se, but the personnel to run, maintain, incorporate, and protect these resources that most mattered. Budget cuts stripped Huerta's staff to the bone. At one of the first board meetings I attended in the district, support staff, teachers, students, and community members packed the boardroom, leaving standing room only, to protest pink slips (layoffs) being given to bus drivers, cafeteria workers, and janitorial staff as part of an effort to cut $1.8 million from the district budget. The following year, the board cut all the school librarians, the locksmith (whose job it was to ensure classrooms could not be broken into and computers stolen), and the technical support staff (in charge of keeping computers working). The board considered cutting bus service for students but worried about liability (particularly because a substantial portion of their budget went to addressing five existing lawsuits). These cuts meant that the supplies that the schools did have—library books, computers, the two projectors, all of which were heavily used—would not have the staff to maintain and protect them. At every meeting, those losing their jobs—often parents, uncles, aunts, and grandparents of the students themselves, as well as those who desperately relied on the services—showed up to protest and plead. I saw board members, also elected from within the community, cry as they sat in their chambers having to make cuts they knew would hurt students and families. In contrast, a couple miles away, just over the freeway, Valley Vista Middle School (Valley Vista) was overflowing with resources.

Valley Vista Middle School

Valley Vista was just off a busy thoroughfare, but otherwise sat amid homes and quiet streets. There was a mural on one wall, painted from digitalized photos of the students. On my first day visiting the school, I was ushered into a room where six middle school students sat, headphones on, monitoring computer flat screens. In front of them, a glass window peeked into a sound studio with multiple TV cameras, a microphone, and two studio chairs. The door to the studio opened and we rushed in. Mr Wilson, the principal, gestured for me to sit next to him in a chair. "Before I start," he addressed the camera, "I want to introduce you to a very special guest who you're going to be seeing around campus. This is Becky Alexander." I waved at the camera and said "hi" as instructed and smiled. "Becky is a graduate student at the University of California and for her research she's going to be working here at Valley Vista Middle School, looking at how you get along with and interact with each other and then following some of you to Westside High." My introduction was transmitted to all the classrooms via closed caption TV while the students learned to operate cameras, control audio and visual outputs, and direct.

I was stunned by the opulence of this encounter. It wasn't simply the technological equipment or the magnitude of putting a professional TV station in a middle school and TVs in all classrooms. Rather, it was having the resources and teachers to train and supervise students, the time and tools to integrate the technology into the overall structure of the school, and the staff to maintain and update all that equipment. I would soon learn that other elective classroom spaces with a similar level of development included a woodshop, photo lab, and computer lab.

While Valley Vista had roughly 25 percent more students than Huerta, they had three times as many teachers working with their eighth-grade students and offered six times as many courses. There were only five eighth-grade teachers at Huerta and 17 at Valley Vista. All Huerta eighth-grade students were placed into two core course offerings (Eighth Grade Core and Eighth Grade Math/Science). At Valley Vista, students chose from at least 17 courses including Eighth Grade Spanish and French, Woodshop, Art, Video, and four levels of math. The science lab course was run by a designated science teacher with full lab equipment. All Huerta students took Algebra I, while Valley Vista students could choose between Middle School Algebra, High School Algebra, and Geometry (a tenth-grade course). The funding for much of this came from a private educational foundation, through which Valley Vista parents contributed over $1 million per year to support the school.

Teachers at Valley Vista described the ample professional development resources they received. Ms Hegel, a newer eighth-grade core teacher, explained "everything that I've asked for, they've been able to do in some way, and it's not about just throwing money at the problem, but it's 'oh, I really want to learn more about this' and so, you know, … here's a book to read … I've been sent to Virginia twice to be trained in differentiated instruction, you know … they're just so supportive and they have the resources … I feel so lucky."

Not only was the school wealthy, but many students were also. They start "in kindergarten knowing they're going to go to college," Ms Hegel explained. She described the vacation homes, lavish extracurriculars, travel, and ample supply of private tutors that nurtured her students. A handful of Glenview students were bused to Valley Vista through a transfer program called Swap that settled a desegregation lawsuit in the early 1980s. The school would otherwise be even more white and almost all upper middle class and wealthy. As it was, the school had a small portable cart from which school lunches were served to the handful of free and reduced lunch recipients.

Students from Huerta and Valley Vista went to high school together at Westside—a blue-ribbon public school of more than 2,000 students that served students from four different cities and more than 16 different schools. Glenview students were dispersed between the four Westside Unified High School District schools as part of a desegregation plan, but the internal tracking and dynamics of the district evidenced the limits of that work. Westside boasted a robust slate of AP courses but was heavily tracked. Five levels of courses—Advanced (AS/AP), Regular (R), Basic (B), Below Basic (BB), and Far Below Basic (FBB)—corresponded to the categories on California State assessments and starkly divided the school, largely by race, class, and neighborhood. While Westside administrators and teachers often blamed Glenview School District (and their purported failures) for the racialized tracking and achievement patterns, teachers, administrators, and families from Glenview worried that, despite the abundant resources at this high school, their students were not being well served.

The transition to high school

When I asked him about the transition to high school, Mr Jackson, an Eighth Grade Core teacher at Huerta, quickly responded, "it's horrible, just horrible." He described endemic failures in communication "like for registration, not a single parent was there for their child to sign up for classes."

Me: Were they invited?

Mr J: I have no idea! I mean, I didn't even really know when the registration people were coming for sure.

Mr Jackson had tried to intervene in the process: "they were putting them all in … support classes so it's like Math, Math, English, English, PE, go home. I literally had to sit there and be like NOOOOOO, he's a better student than that! That seventh-grade test score doesn't show who he is now! I really had to advocate for them," he continued "'cause the kids were just sitting there wide eyed … 'hey strange white lady circling things on paper.'" Mr. Jackson hadn't been able to get a sub for that day, so he had to leave his class alone for periods of time in order to be in these meetings; "…it was such a horrible day."

Mr Jackson's advocacy was shaped by what happened in his first year teaching at Huerta. He hadn't understood the system. "I was like one of the kids, watching them circle all these things," he said, but when his students came back they told him "how much they HATE it … how they've got all Fs … I was like, there's no way I'm going to let that happen to these kids again, and so I really pushed for them to get these good classes." Mr Jackson visited Westside High School to see what his students experienced. He vividly recounted the tracking. He saw a mostly white English class studying Shakespeare: "it was very, like, well structured and everybody was on point." Then, he "went to a support reading class and it looked very similar to my class as far as color goes" but "the teacher just stood up there at the front and just talked, talked, talked." He imagined for the students "it was just kind of like, 'I don't care about this teacher, this teacher doesn't care about me, I'm just going to bide my time…that was just hard to watch."

Other Huerta teachers expressed similar frustration with the transition. "The communication is really bare bones," Mr Billings, the other core teacher, told me. Westside officials came to his class to present, but "there were no visuals and there were these ladies or men standing and talking. The kids had no idea really what they were talking about." He said that his students, when they do come back, "don't really have much to say. Usually, they're embarrassed to talk about it. Oftentimes they've had bad experiences." He told the story of one student who was failing Geometry because he kept missing the bus. "You know, kids come back and they say, 'I'm getting Cs, Ds, Fs,' I've never had a student come back and say, like, 'I'm doing stellar.' They've got to be embarrassed," he went on, "they're not in the high classes, they don't feel successful, they're taking low grades."

Mr Billings had met with leaders from one of the high schools at the district office to talk about how unfair the system was. He suggested it might be better if, at minimum, students from individual schools in Glenview were kept together at the same high school so they could stay in community with one another. Even better, he thought, all the students from Glenview should go to the same school, since "kids cannot buy into the community, cannot buy into something." He went on, "if you want the families of Glenview to, like, own their children's education, you should make it easier for them to be involved. That means it should be somewhere that they can walk to, somewhere close and all together." The PE teacher simply told me, "You have to write about this! And you have to do a god job!"

The contrast between Huerta teachers' concerns and the glowing way Valley Vista Middle School teachers described the transition was dramatic and unsettling. Ms Hegel reflected on how academically prepared her students felt: "they'll say they feel so prepared … so on top of things, they totally get it … I hear really good things about the kids that go on … a lot of them … just, find their stride … it just brings tears to my eyes because I'm like, you finally got it, and you finally have found, you know, who you are." She attributed this success to the work of the school, saying "I feel like we have really, really high expectations ... maybe to the point of being too extreme ... I don't take excuses, I don't deal with any of the stuff."

Valley Vista Middle School students all went to Westside High School unless they opted for private school. Mrs Hegel reflected on how "Valley Vista Middle kids really bond with each other in a way." While they had cliques in middle school, she heard that in high school they "would just all sit together and they were this big blob ... they've found this comfort and they've found these friends that they love and it's like a support system for them." As she talked it was clear she was describing a particular sub-set of her students, those who called themselves the "popular kids."

Ms Hegel didn't feel like she had much initial understanding of the placement process. "I realized my first year I was just scrambling." Unclear on the difference between levels, she just placed all 50 students in honors or AS courses. Following this experience, she, like Mr Jackson, spent a day shadowing. The AS classes resonated with her, "I was like, this is just like the way I teach ... that's a lot of what Valley Vista is and the teachers ... just expect the kids to do what they're supposed to do." She contrasted this to the regular class where "it's a lot of the same material and the same concepts but it's a lot more ... added instruction, in a way." She added that in the regular classes "they find a few ways to teach things, whereas in AS it's like, you get it, move on, or you have to figure out a way to find it out by yourself." She did not visit support classes as she did not anticipate any of her students being placed there.

I asked her about her students' experiences coming together with kids from different schools. "I hear a lot more from parents," she said. "They're worried about their kid, you know … being with the masses or being in such a diverse school where it's so dangerous and stuff like that." She was skeptical about parents' concerns: "you have got to be kidding me …. Think about what goes on in the private schools. I hear stories about parties and drugs … these are high school kids, they're all morons." But she had heard the high school was "really divided. I mean," she said, dropping her tone, "I think it's like the white kids and the minority kids, whatever the groupings might be … Tongan or Hispanic or African American, whatever it is. It's definitely a stigma … you know, white kids, they're in AS and it's da, da, da. I guess I shouldn't only say white but it's sadly the majority, you know, all the Valley Vista … kids, they go to AS, they go straight A, they do this and all the other kids don't. There's a total division [but] you can't expect them to, I mean it's not always a Lifetime movie where they're gonna be best friends."

This book

This book takes up where these teachers' questions leave off. What were young people's experiences as they transitioned from these middle schools to Westside High? How did they make sense of themselves, their communities, and one another in the process? What did this inequality mean to them and how did they navigate, contest, and participate in it? This book tells the stories of eight young people and the communities and contexts that surrounded them as they made the transition from these racially isolated middle schools into this desegregated but deeply divided and inequitable high school. Four students (Memo, Khalil, Jaqueline, and Rahul) were from Huerta and four (Cam, Amy, Talli, and Jonathan) were from Valley Vista. I began my research during their second semester of eighth grade, at their middle schools. The book follows the students as they begin ninth grade at Westside High School. The historical and ongoing formation of the deep race-class lines that students of color, in particular, had to navigate—in the school, the neighborhood, and beyond—are central to understanding how injustice permeated and was reproduced and contested in these schools. Each chapter focuses on one of the students, exploring their ninth-grade experience in relation to their middle-school years and ending with an epilogue based on their reflections several years later. The final chapter shares the story of Elijah, an artist, community organizer, and former Westside student from Glenview who I met after he graduated. His story expands the conversation out to think more broadly about Glenview as a pedagogical space.

Some notes on my frames and language

To think through these contexts, I use a critical race-class perspective (Leonardo, 2012). This lens understands race and class at the intersection between different interlocking systems—white supremacy, coloniality, and capitalism. Race is a socially constructed category. This means that a certain set of chosen physical characteristics that have no special meaning on their own were given social, political, legal, and ideological relevance in order to create differences in rights, privileges, and power

(Leonardo, 2009). Whiteness, as a category, was constructed from people wildly diverse in their linguistic, religious, political, and economic backgrounds as a means of determining who would be defined as fully human—fully eligible for the rights of personhood and property. Capitalism as a political–economic system thrives and depends upon class inequality and racialization and has been a key tool in producing this subjugation. One way this has happened is through the provision of whiteness as a form of privilege that gives white people some limited social power even when they don't have economic power, thus limiting inter-racial solidarity in resisting unjust economic conditions (Roediger, 2007). Whiteness is a socially constructed category (Perry, 2002), but unlike Blackness, it "does not describe a group with a sense of common experiences or kindship outside of acts of colonization and terror" (Dumas, 2016). Coloniality as a system links capitalism and white supremacy, justifying the seizure and occupation of land; mass displacement, murder, exploitation, and torture; and theft of resources (Quijano, 2000). It justifies such practices as compatible with democracy through racio-ideological logics that structure Black people, Indigenous people, and people of color as less than fully human (Grande, 2018).

BIPOC (Black, Indigenous, and people of color) is an important language construction for talking about the interconnected ways people have been subject to racial and colonial oppression and engaged in resistance, without conflating different forms of historic and contemporary structural violence (Grady, 2020). In this text, however, I primarily use "people of color," naming specific groups when I am talking about that group. This is a slightly older construct but is the one both people in Glenview and scholars were using at the time I did my work. It emerged, following the phrase "women of color," out of coalitional organizing as a way to construct common struggle in resistance to white supremacy (Moraga and Anzaldua, 1983). More recently, scholars and organizers have been attentive to the urgency of holding space for coalition while recognizing how systems of oppression like antiblackness (Dumas and Ross, 2016) and settler colonial occupation (Tuck and Yang, 2012) affect people differently depending on their own group histories with racial capitalism (Robinson, 2019) and may require different organizing strategies. BIPOC opens up this complexity, but I don't use it until the end of this text because it wasn't the frame people were using at the time. One of the challenges with using BIPOC is not misusing it in ways that occlude the specificity it is intended to add or bring back to the fore. Many Pacific Islanders identify as First Nations peoples, and many Black and Latinx students have Indigenous ancestry (for example, Memo, as he got older, sometimes identified as Indigenous, tracing his Purepecha roots), but I also don't want to misrepresent the extent to which indigeneity is represented in this text or context. The specificity of antiblackness can also get occluded when BIPOC is used to collapse group identities.

I sometimes use Black and Brown, which, again, is a common organizing construct, often used to talk about organizing against shared circumstances Black and Latinx folks grapple with. The construct is particularly salient in Black and Brown Power movements and movements to collaborate for racial justice (Irizarry and Rosa, 2015). The use of Brown is sometimes expanded to non-Black communities of color more broadly; particularly, people who self-identify as Brown. I use Brown in a way similar to "of color," following Bettina Love's (2019) usage. I primarily use the term Black to refer to people racialized as such, because it points towards the constructed nature of the category and is globally inclusive. Black is capitalized and white is not because Black describes a social connection grounded in something other than privilege. I do occasionally use African American if I know that is what somebody prefers to be called or it feels more respectful, for example when I am first introducing someone before I know how they prefer to identify. African American is used primarily for people from the United States, and in some cases throughout the Americas, whose ancestry descends from Africa. Both terms, although contested, emerge out of generations of organizing and movement work focused on self-definition; honoring African roots, lineages, traditions, knowledges, and frameworks that long precede colonization and enslavement; and recognizing how Blackness functions as both a racial construct or racial project and a space of global, diasporic collective organizing, cultural production, and knowledge generation (Ogbar, 2019). What people prefer to be called is tied to their personal and political preferences and to the extent possible I endeavor to follow these preferences.

I use Latina, Latino, and Latinx to refer to people with heritage tracing to Latin America, depending on what I know about how they identify and prefer to be referenced. When I am speaking, I use Latinx. At the time of my research, I would have used Latino/a or Latin@ to be gender inclusive but these are both in a binary, whereas Latinx is constructed to include all genders and can indicate broader boundary work (Torres, 2018). Latinx is an ethnicity, in which people are racialized in different ways.

People can be Latinx and white, Black, Indigenous, and they can be from a wide range of countries, languages, and religions. Many Latinx people have mixed ancestry that includes African, European, and Indigenous descent and identify as mestizo or mixed. Some Mexican-American Latinx people trace their roots to land (still Indigenous land), stretching from the US/Mexico border to Wyoming, that the US occupied and Mexico ceded in the Treaty of Guadalupe Hidalgo. US promises to respect Mexican land rights were disregarded throughout California and other seized territories as courts and police refused to prosecute white squatters or uphold the rights of Mexican landholders. The phrase "we didn't cross the border, the border crossed us" describes this relationship of occupation and displacement (Acuña, 2014).

I use both Asian and Asian-American in the text, depending on how individuals identify. Much of the broader discourse refers to Asians as a racial category, which includes people of Asian descent who, like members of other racialized groups, could have had ancestors in the US since long before the declaration of independence or could have recently arrived. Asian-Americans are diverse in language, religion, time of arrival, national ancestry, and class. The socially constructed category, again, largely has to do with how people have been racialized in the US and by US immigration policy and how they have united in struggle against mutual oppression (Takaki, 1990). Pacific Islander and Polynesian are clumped with Asian in census categories but racialized differently in the US. I use these terms, Polynesian and Pacific Islander, interchangeably, as did people in this study, to refer to people from Tonga, Samoa, Fiji, and other Pacific Islands. While many customs are shared across the islands, different languages, colonial histories, and traditions also make this a constructed category (Labrador and Wright, 2011)

Racial analysis is vital for describing how white supremacy functions and people grapple individually and collectively with racism across class divides, but it can also occlude critical relations of class and power within groups and across racialized groups. Race and class intersect because of the histories described above. Black, Latinx, Indigenous, Pacific Islander, and some Asian groups make up a disproportionate share of those in poverty, with negative economic wealth or without access to well-paying jobs and higher education. Wealth and whiteness are concentrated together, as are social and political power in the US. These are broad patterns, rooted in political policy and social practice, and tell important stories about inequality. There are also important stories they leave out. Most Black, Latinx, Pacific Islander, and Asian people in the US are middle class or above, despite garnering lower wages than whites, and over 40% of people living in poverty in the US are white. The white families described in this book are very wealthy and in no way representative of white people in general. Similarly, even though many families in Glenview struggle, only 25 percent are officially below the poverty line and many are middle class. Other more solidly middle class and elite Black and Brown suburbs exist elsewhere (Patillo, 2013). There are people of also color from across the class spectrum living in Westside and other majority white suburbs and white people of various class statuses living in Glenwood and other majority-of-color communities. The polarization of race and class in this context is, however, similar to that in many other urban and suburban contexts where service economies bring white wealth and working people of color together.

I draw on four core concepts to help me understand these young people's experiences, identity construction, and the spaces and places they were a part of. These are: displacement, (de)segregation, dispossession, and the frontier. Each concept describes a particular kind of structural violence or harm that helps situate these young people's stories through a critical race-class lens. Discussion of each concept is embedded throughout the text as "learning objectives." As I discuss each learning objective, I also elaborate on the creative, generative ways people, including youth, respond to, resist, and rework these violences. I highlight language, concepts, and theories that help show both the depth of what is lost and harmed, but also the persistence, survival, resilience, resistance, defiance, and regenerative capacity of people, schools, and communities in the face of persistent displacement, segregation, and dispossession.

Context of the work

I worked in Glenview and Westside schools in the late 1990s. I returned in 2007 and worked and lived in these communities for five more years[2]. I returned for follow-up interviews and to meet with and interview Glenview community activists, older youth, elders, and organizers in 2017. I have lived and worked in both communities described in this book. My understanding of the dynamics I describe is partial and forever growing, but what I have learned has primarily come from combining the theoretical tools described in this book with close observation, or deep hanging out, with young people and interviews with them, teachers, parents, and community members. I also spent time in the archives—both in libraries and online—studying the history of these schools and communities, tracing ways people have fought for and against educational equality and how the broader politics of race and place in and beyond these neighborhoods shaped that struggle.

This book shares the pieces of each of the eight focal students' lives I was able to witness during my time spent with them. As I tell these stories, I draw on the broader histories of and relations between these schools and their communities, as documented in literature, archives, and elder testimony, to help illuminate how these individual stories are connected to one another and to broader structures. Each of these young people is unique and precious and their lives far exceed the tiny glimpses I had into them. I have done my best to represent how I see and understand what they shared with me and what I saw as I spent these years with them. Studying this context and learning from and with these young people has helped me better understand school (de)segregation as a socially situated and deeply contextualized relation—one intimately tied to shifting racialized relations of power and domination.

A close look at these schools and students disrupts the good white school, bad brown school narrative that underlies much of the public imagination about desegregation (Siddle Walker, 1996), or educational inequality in general. It illuminates the radical, creative, imaginative, passionate, and relentless educational, pedagogical, and care work engaged by Black and Brown educational and community leaders, families, children, and residents in Glenview. The resource hoarding and segregation by white communities and ways whiteness operated in educational spaces, impoverishing the curriculum, content, and learning opportunities, raise broad questions about what is meant by education and where it makes sense to look for models. At the same time, the realities of deep resource and opportunity gaps and the politics of the educational spaces belie easy romantic answers. The young people, and their sense making, help illuminate that complexity while also making crystal clear the injustices they experience and in which they participate.

Positionality

No one enters a space from a position of neutrality. We are connected to and figured within contexts and relations we might seek to understand and represent and are always working from some particular point of view and set of experiences. What we see and hear is also shaped by how others perceive and understand us—how they read our bodies, language, and movements in socio-political-historical context (Villenas, 1996). The stories of the white students in this text remind me in many ways of my own, despite our different social class positions. The tools for critical and racial analysis I use in this work, that let me think critically about whiteness, I learned primarily through intensive dialogue with scholars of color and critical white scholars (who in turn learned from scholars and organizers of color), as well as through intensive reading of work by the same. Still, my white middle-classness shaped every aspect of this project. Although I lived in Glenview for two years, with Mexican-American and Salvadoran friends who had much longer relationships with the city, I was clearly not from there. Students and adults spoke to me as an outsider and a white person. They would say things like "no offense" before saying something about "white people." When I moved into Glenview or traveled in Glenview, I was often conscious of how my whiteness stood out. The liberal colorblind racist frameworks I was immersed in growing up would tell me my whiteness made me vulnerable but I knew from study (of both texts and social reality) that my whiteness actually afforded innumerable protections. The same dynamics of racist policing, criminalization, and dispossession that targeted Black, Latinx, and Islander Glenview residents functioned for my protection.

I had no firsthand knowledge of what young people growing up in Glenview experienced, except what I witnessed from the young people I worked with and their loved ones and families. I was raised amid and struggled to understand the type of borders, frontiers, and dynamics described here from my own location: one grounded in white flight, liberal colorblind racism, and white savior fantasies. By the time I did this work I was much more deeply attuned to my own racial violence—how my white body, actions, and words could do racial damage and harm regardless of my intent—and how I was part of the dynamics I sought to understand. My presence in Glenview, no matter how justice-minded or solidarity-driven, was part of the dynamics of the frontier, as I had the freedom to cross and uncross boundaries, take up in and leave neighborhoods, educate, and be framed as expert on a city I have known for only a heartbeat.

I have endeavored to keep my attention on the relational dynamics between these cities, schools, and young people. I approach the young people in this study from a place of deep humility and try not to say who they are or what they believe, or to act as expert on their cultures, needs, aspirations, identities, or selves; I only got tiny glimpses of these young people and am certainly in no position to frame and fix their existence. Nor do I present what they told me as some absolute truth. They would likely tell you a different story about their story than the one I have told. This book is my analysis, with the tools I had at my disposal, of what I saw and heard over the two years they let me into their lives.

The students

The four young people I worked with from Huerta were all friends. Their allegiances to and relationships with one another shifted throughout the course of this project, but they all knew and cared about one another. Khalil and Rahul were best friends, had been since fifth grade, and continued as such despite huge differences between them. Khalil was African American, short, clean-cut, outgoing, kind, cheerful, and studious. He lived in a loving, tightknit household with his mother and sister in a small one-bedroom apartment. They had survived homeless for periods of time. Rahul was a tall, lanky, Fijian student with long hair, and the shadow of a mustache. He lived alone in a large house with his father who often traveled for work. He was often cared for by his large network of extended family and was particularly close with his sister and cousin. Both Khalil and Rahul had strong school records and scored at or above grade level in math and English. While Rahul had begun to get in trouble and focus less on school by the time I met him, his friends and teachers remembered when he had been among the strongest students at Huerta.

Jaqueline was close friends with both Khalil and Rahul. An A-student, member of the dance team, and very popular, Jaqueline was known for her bright colors and gregarious personality. She lived in a with her mother, who she thought of as one of her best friends, and brothers who she deeply loved and relied on. Her father was incarcerated and facing possible deportation. Memo was friends with Jaqueline and the other Huerta students. He had been separated from his parents for many years and had crossed the US–Mexico border when he was ten years old. His family of six, including his mom and baby siblings who he cherished, had caved out space for themselves in the living room of his uncle's one-bedroom apartment. Memo was also a very strong student, scoring at or above grade level in math but still, when I began shadowing him, labeled and placed as Limited English Proficient (LEP)[3]. Khalil and Memo's families were both facing intense poverty and instability, while Jaqueline's was slightly more economically secure and Rahul's solidly lower-middle class.

Valley Vista had much more clearly defined social groups than Huerta and, as most students transferred to Westside, these groups tended to stay intact. Amy, who was white, and Jonathan, who was Asian American, were both part of Amy called the "drama" group. As she compared them to other groups at her middle school: "they're the people that … wear Juicy and are just classic mean girls … we're sort of the, uh, the whoever doesn't make it there can hang out with us. Just, it's the everybody clique." Jonathan, a fourth generation Chinese-American student, loved acting and debating and was in very advanced courses. He lived with his parents in a house in Westside. Amy was a student who worked hard and struggled to stay in advanced courses. She seemed sincere and open and was known as a reliable friend. She counted her mother as her best friend and lived with her mother and father in a large house in Westside.

Cam and Talli, both white, were part of different groups of students. Cam's group were generally recognized as the "popular" kids. Extremely outgoing, he had a large family and spacious home in the hills. He was a student who seemed to get high A's without trying and his father was a leader of a successful company. Talli also lived in the wealthiest part of Westside[4]. Unlike other students from Westside, however, in middle school she largely hung out with students of color who were transfer students from Glenview. Grappling with her mother's alcoholism, she struggled to keep up academically and had perhaps the worst middle school academic record of any student in this book. Cam, Talli, and Amy were all wealthy whereas Jonathan was upper-middle class.

As they transitioned to high school, some of the students from the different schools came to know each other. Cam, Rahul, and Khalil were all in the same Geometry class, and Amy and Memo took World Studies together. Jaqueline became friends with Cam's girlfriend and invited them both to her Quinciñera, and Cam, as a member of the homecoming court, seemed known by everybody. As these students entered high school they were forced to reflect, some more than others, on inequality in these schools and communities. They had, without much help from adults, to make sense of the differences between the middle schools, the glaring wealth divides, the racialized tracking, and their relationships with one another. They did all this in the midst of the 2007–2008 sub-prime crisis that wracked communities like

Glenview, causing massive housing instability and wealth losses (Oliver and Shapiro, 2008). In some cases, what was happening in Glenview—the gentrification, predatory equity schemes, gutting of social protections, and housing losses—seemed to parallel what was happening at the school. Glenview students and those who cared for them were fighting with all they had to protect families and loved ones, hold onto precious resources (linguistics, cultures, community, knowledges, and so on) as they toggled between contexts that were under-resourced but racially protective and opulent and steeped in whiteness. Meanwhile Westside students, while they had glimpses into their own privilege that provoked questioning, also actively deployed their advantage, largely, as their educational spaces encouraged them to, defining themselves as those who cared, deserved, knew, tried, and behaved. Each chapter of this book addresses a different students' story, interwoven with interviews with family, community, educators, and peers to tease out how they made sense of and were enmeshed within these schools and communities.

Learning objective: Displacement

These first two chapters, Jaqueline and Memo, interrogate processes of place-making and displacement. Many of the young people from Glenview experienced persistent displacement. They were compelled to leave their childhood homes and countries; were evicted or forced to move; experienced homelessness and housing insecurity; and were placed outside of their linguistic, cultural, and social contexts. In order to know what displacement means, however, we have to be able to think about what place means. The way I think about place is influenced by critical geographers, feminists of color, and Indigenous scholars. In these understandings, place is not a container or property, but rather something constructed, made, and lived. Place-making entails labor—that of humans and others. Often the labor of crafting "homeplaces" —(hooks, 1997) safer pedagogical, political, and restorative places amid violently oppressive circumstances and relations—is done by women, and women of color in particular. Displacement goes hand in hand with this endless reconstruction of place and the usurpation of the labor involved in place-making.

As you read the next two chapters, think about the following four questions. In these chapters:

1) Who are the various actors and what are the various actions you see involved in "making places"? In what ways do you see this place-making affecting education?
2) What different kinds of displacement do you see happening? Are there ways you might even see some of what is happening in the classroom as displacement? Explain.

3) Why do you think it might matter to think about place-making and displacement as one part of thinking about segregation?
4) How have you and/or your ancestors been displaced or participated in and/or contributed to the displacement of others in communities, schools, or beyond (whether or not this was done intentionally)?

1
Memo: This school is for the white kids

I was sitting in the back of Memo's freshman (first year of high school) World Studies class. It was the day of Barack Obama's presidential inauguration, January 20, 2008. As I looked over at him next to me, I noticed that Memo's head was newly shaved; he looked taller. His grandfather died only a few days prior. Because he was undocumented, Memo could not travel to Mexico for the funeral. He and his family mourned from a distance. For Memo, who lived with his grandparents between the ages of six and ten after his mother left for the US, the loss was particularly hard. He had been unable to see them since he crossed the border, buried on the floor of the backseat of a stranger's car, four years ago. He missed them horribly. Now his grandfather was gone and he could not go say goodbye.

Mr Howard, Memo's teacher, was trying to lead the class in a discussion of the significance of Obama's election. What would they "take away" from this moment? There were 26 students—ten white, eight Latinx, six Black, and two Asian and Pacific Islander. They sat in two rectangles, facing one another, with an aisle down the middle that ended in a podium. Mr Howard moved between the blocks of students. If he turned to look at either side, his back was to the other. Jaqueline and Jamie were in this class, and they sat with their backs to the door, as did Memo and I, and as did most of the white students. The year prior, Mr Howard's first year at Westside, freshman World Studies classes had been de-tracked. Two classes—regular and AS—were collapsed into one. The sides of the room felt like remnants of the tracking pattern. Jaqueline would later point out to me that not only were the sides of the room split, but the students of color who did sit on the door-side (the white side) always sat in the back.

The school had de-tracked World Studies because, as Mr Howard put it, there was "basically no integration of any kind." Tracking was notoriously difficult to dismantle at Westside High even though teachers and administrators worried about how it facilitated inequality. When classes are tracked, students are separated by purported ability into different levels of classes (Oakes, 2005). Tracking is designed to allow for differentiation of teaching to meet different levels of ability, but in practice, it is a form of internal segregation that produces schools within a school, communicates harmful messages about young people's capacities, denies some students—often poor students and students of color—access to rigorous academic resources, and prevents modes of teaching and learning that bridge and interrogate difference. Nonetheless, multiple prior attempts at de-tracking at Westside had been met with resistance, primarily from white and wealthy parents.

Mr Howard described mixed feelings about the decision to have only one level of freshman World Studies: "As an educator it's really frustrating at times." He taught a unit on globalization the year prior and "came in with the assumption that these kids would know how to use an atlas." Half the class did, he said, because they learned it five years ago, and "the other half wasn't aware of what latitude and longitude were." This difference in familiarity with the standard tools of geography was not surprising. Opportunity gaps (Ladson-Billings, 2006) pervaded these schools as they did nationally, particularly where teacher shortages, standards and testing pressures, and lack of materials narrowed the curriculum. Huerta students were struggling with multiple displacements and ongoing mobility that made curricular consistency difficult and their teachers often triaged to focus on test score gains in dominant subjects.

At the same time, reading an atlas is the easy part of geography. What many students from Glenview did have that their peers from Westside largely did not was intimate knowledge of multiple geographies, experiences with surviving globalization-induced displacement and dispossession, and multi-lingual and multi-cultural lives. These "funds of knowledge," valuable knowledge not recognized in schools (Moll and Amanti, 1992), were much more difficult to teach or understand than how to use a map, but were untapped in Mr Howard's class.

Reflecting on Glenview students' hidden geographical or "worldly" knowledge, I was reminded of a math class I sat in on the year prior at Huerta. Mr Girard's class was graphing inequalities, making books about journeys they had taken or would take. I was sitting near a table of four boys. Daniel, a Black student who was very good at math, was struggling with this assignment. He had an E40 hoodie pulled up over his head most of the way. He stared at his paper, imagining places to take a trip to. Other students were talking about going to Tonga and Mexico. At the table with Daniel were two Latino students: Hugo and Miguel. Hugo was drawing a picture of his trip to Mexico. On the page were cactuses and the desert and the sun. Miguel turned to him:

Miguel: That's not Mexico.

Hugo: It's not?

Miguel: Even in the desert that's not what Mexico looks like. It's advanced!

Another student, Mele, began talking about her trip to Tonga, and Ita, another Tongan student, began debating the length of the plane ride with her. Meanwhile, Mr Girard helped Daniel, who like some students may never have traveled outside of Glenview, tap into his journeys within his own community.

Mr Girard: You need to just choose somewhere, it could be anywhere, you could go to the corner store or …

Daniel: I'll go to my grandma's house!

Mr Girard: Okay, perfect, to your grandma's house.

Many Glenview students led bi- or tri-national existences. Many were multi-lingual. Often their displacement, as in Memo's case, was fueled by "globalization", whether they understood that yet or not. Others had not left Glenview, whether because of lack of resources (time, money, means), fears of vulnerability to different forms of state and interpersonal violence, or for other reasons. But even those young people who did not have experience from outside of Glenview lived in a diverse, complex, multi-cultural community where they learned about and through the lives of their peers. They also had intimate knowledge of borders and their own geographies, whether those were neighborhood or national, and a complex understanding of the roles these played in shaping social processes. This Huerta math class did a better job incorporating this knowledge than a Westside class dedicated to this topic. Mr Howard identified unidirectional gaps in student knowledge. He neither identified these an injustice, nor recognized the geographical richness and academic capacities many of his Glenview students brought with them (or the limits of the knowledge of his Westside students)—for him, the "good" students were the white and wealthy students.

Mr Howard's deficit narrative

Mr Howard described that moment with the atlas as the moment he began to understand the stratification of the school he taught in. He characterized it unidirectionally, conflating low test scores with behavior, implying lower-tracked students were a problem. "Imagine having a class of 30 kids ... who all have behavioral issues or outside of school things where it's gang problems or a lot of family concerns, like they take care of their brothers or sisters or things like that. It could be less learning and more babysitting." Instead of recognizing students' labor and resilience (Love, 2019), taking care of loved ones and grappling complex family situations, he saw these as problems. Mr Howard expressed a logic that was shared by many white teachers, administrators, and students and also pervasive in much policy and scholarly work—the idea that the goal of desegregation was for Black and Brown children to "be exposed to and internalize white middle-class norms and values" (Glicken and Miller, 1992, p. 21) through contact with white middle-class kids. Mr Howard speculated that "Maybe," with detracking, the habits of high-tracked students "will rub off on [those in lower tracks] and improve them." He believed the kids "who are already academically advanced … understand that they are here almost to … be a mentor for some of the students that need a model." He seemed unable to see, let alone imagine, Westside students had anything to learn from the students of color in the room, their families, the educators who had supported them thus far, or their broader communities; not their knowledge, skills, capacities, or perseverance. His words reiterated common lenses through which students of color are viewed by educators and in much education literature—deficit and damage (Tuck, 2009)—and set himself and the white students in the room up as saviors.

Mr Howard didn't know much of anything about Memo, his family, his history, his friends, or prior schooling. He didn't know how deeply he was mourning, nor the care, love and teaching his grandparents had shared with him. As school staff commonly did with students' relations from Glenview, he assumed Memo's relations were all a hindrance to Memo's academics. He imagined, without irony, that students who lived in mansions, had multiple tutors, and were often cared for by the parents of Glenview youth could model a work ethic for Memo. "Now he's admitted to me that he's been lazy … that's a sign that he doesn't have that push outside of the classroom, like somebody that is constantly looking over his shoulder." Memo was an A/B student in this and all his other classes despite all he was grappling with, but Mr Howard said, "the kids that are getting all A's or As and Bs are the ones that have that, you know, push at home … when he's in a classroom like this, and he's with a good group of students, he's right there with them, and he's smart enough."

The words were meant as a compliment, but failed to recognize the extraordinary private resources that buffeted the students he characterized as "good," the immense labor under incredibly difficult circumstances of Memo and his family and friends in pursuit of his education, and the incredible talent and drive Memo brought to his work.

Like many immigrant parents, Memo's mother, Angelica's, decision to migrate centered around the well-being of her children (Mangual Figueroa, 2011; Dreby, 2010). She agonized over the decision to leave Memo and his sister in Mexico, and over the decision to bring them to the US four years later. *"Dejé a Memo, dejé a Cecilia, me vine, todo a manos de Dios."* ("I left Memo, I left Cecilia, and I came, completely in God's hands.") Memo's trip to the US was dangerous and difficult and meant separation from his grandparents and deep adjustments on arrival (Villegas and Villegas, 2019; Abrego, 2014), but his mom hoped it would create opportunities for him to get an education, something his older siblings had to forgo to work in the fields.

In the living room of Memo's uncle's small apartment, his parents hung sheets from the ceiling to carve out some privacy. Memo, his mom and dad, and his three younger sisters slept on couches and mattresses on the floor. His uncle conducted business from his apartment, so people were in and out day and night, but Memo's mom worked hard to ensure the children stuck to a strict routine. They did chores, sat down at the table together to do homework, and read from the bible. Angelica was determined that her children should succeed in school. She hoped education would offer her children a way to *"salir adelante"* ("get ahead"). She also hoped that their success would provide some cushion against deportation. Nonetheless, they lived with the persistent threat of further displacement (DeGenova, 2002; Desmond, 2016). Immigration and Customs Enforcement (ICE) had knocked down the door of their next-door neighbors the year prior. The apartment they lived in was facing rent spikes as the landlord was waging a predatory equity scheme to undermine rent control and flip the buildings. Employment insecurity, childcare demands, and the need to remit funds to support family still in Mexico also left them economically insecure.

Memo's mom explained how she supported him as he struggled to adjust to schooling in the US. "*Yo le decía mira tu puedes, y me sentaba a la mesa y que hace la tarea y, y a motivarlo para que el la hiciera, el es bien responsable con su tarea.*" ("I told him 'look, you can do it,' and I sat at the table while he did his homework, to motivate him to do it; he is really responsible with his homework.") She hadn't had access to education: "*No habia oportunidad, para que nos daba de comer o con los estudios.*" ("There wasn't any opportunity, we could either eat or study.") She had learned to read in the US by reading her Bible, but assured me, "*En mi familia nadie, nunca, se había graduado.*" ("Nobody in my family had ever graduated.") She was very proud of Memo, and of his siblings: "*Estoy orgullosa de mis hijos,*" ("I'm proud of my children"). She was proud of how hard they worked and of the people they were, how they helped around the house, and how polite they were. Memo was the first in the family to graduate eighth grade, and she was confident he would be the first to graduate high school. She knew this possibility was the result of the sacrifices she had made by separating from him, daring to cross the border, and through their struggle to persist amid such difficult conditions: "*era tanto, era tanto,*" ("it was so much, so much,") she remembered, "*yo tenía que sacarles a mis hijos adelante, tenía que llevarme,*" ("I had to help my children get ahead, I had to go.")

This school is for the white kids

When I interviewed Memo about his transition to high school, he said, "It's fine. The only thing I don't like is that this school is for the white kids." I asked what he meant, and he said, "it's just, it's mostly white kids." I pushed back, saying there were just as many Latinos as white students at the school. "No," he insisted, "it's mostly white." Memo didn't have a precise analysis of how the school was for the white kids, but he knew he could feel the school was "for" them and, whatever their actual percent of the student body, their presence dominated. Jaqueline made a similar percentage distortion in talking about this World Studies class period, saying "almost the whole class was all white." Watching the world studies class that day and talking to Mr Howard, it was easy to see where Memo and Jaqueline were coming from.

As a result of tracking, despite Westside High being "desegregated" and "diverse", there were few classroom spaces where students from across race-class divides were in the same room as one another, let alone in dialogue. Mr Howard tried to make these dialogues happen. But, while he could (and did) analyze systems of power and valorize struggles against injustice globally and historically, he struggled to see them in his own classroom or among his own students. Despite the fact that he acknowledged resource divides, he did not see the long history of anti-oppressive organizing in Glenview, nor recognize how he and his students were steeped in the structures—coloniality, white supremacy—he critiqued through his curriculum (Patel, 2016). When he addressed these injustices, they were in the past, in the South, or in another country. Mr Howard began the semester with a study of anti-apartheid and anti-colonial movements, regularly tried to engage students in discussion, and brought in current events. But, despite the seemingly anti-racist content, the actual class dynamics reinforced whiteness.

Whiteness in the classroom

As class began on inauguration day, Mr Howard initiated a discussion: "What will you take away from today?" he asked the room. The first three students to raise their hands were white women, all of whom talked about this election as a symbol of racial progress. The fourth was also white, dressed in designer jeans and a white cotton shirt, her light blonde hair tied back in a ponytail. "Yes?" Mr Howard called on her. She began haltingly "Well, there are, like, some people in my family who were, like, born in the 20s who, like, wouldn't vote for Obama because he was, like, because he was Black…" There was an audible sound of "aw no!" and a hissing noise as four Black students, sitting in the chairs opposite her, facing her, inhaled through their teeth and shifted in their chairs.

Mr Howard quieted them quickly "wait, wait and hear what she has to say!" He moved his body between them and the girl and extended his hand out toward them in a *stop, calm down* gesture, palm facing their direction, implying the Black students were disruptive or even threatening. "Go on," he coaxed. The girl was now facing only Mr Howard, her voice so quiet it was impossible to hear from only a few seats away. She appeared intimidated by the reaction from across the room. Mr Howard let her finish, then tried to translate her words for the class: "What I think she's saying is that for people who are older, who have lived through a time when there was segregation, that this has more meaning for them … this is a moment that shows just how much we have overcome."

Following this students' remarks and the tension that accompanied them, there was silence in the classroom. Mr Howard waited. Nobody raised their hands. The students who had reacted when the girl first spoke now stared not at Mr Howard, but past him, their bodies slouched back in their chairs and their gazes averted. "Does anyone else have anything to add?" Mr Howard prompted after a few moments of silence. "Anyone?" Then, without acknowledging the earlier interrupted, but not failed, attempt by Black students to contribute to the discussion (for indeed, there was a contribution), Mr Howard called them out: "There are only three people who have talked so far and they are all, um, from a non-minority group. Do any of you from other groups have anything to say?" Silence.

I asked Mr Howard about this conversation later. He thought there had been a "misinterpretation of what she was saying." He explained, "there's still people in this country who … adhere to that, that racial agenda and I thought it was good that she brought it up." It wasn't clear what he thought was misinterpreted. "I think some of the minority kids, obviously on the other side of the room, kind of got a little upset about that," he went on, "at the same time, they didn't want to speak up either and that [I] was kind of disappointed by them not being willing to, you know, speak up in class." When these students had spoken, Mr

Howard had implied—with his body, his shushing, and later with his words—that he thought they were confused and aggressive. He silenced them, then he critiqued their silence. Mr Howard, despite discussing racist threats against Obama, followed frames for understanding race that were dominant at Westside High— racism was bad, but was mostly about "a few people" who still "adhered to" something antiquated, meanwhile his Black students, in response to the implication they were disruptive, used one of the strategies Black people have historically used to protect their safety amid white racial violence—they stayed silent and averted their gaze.

Mr Howard concluded the lesson with a discussion of Obama's call for service on Martin Luther King's birthday. He asked if anyone would bring toiletries and other items for the backpacks for the homeless project. "I would," Memo answered. "You would Memo, really?"

"Yeah," Memo replied.

When I talked to Mr Howard later about Memo, he used this moment as an example of Memo's big heart. "Memo is," he said, "I think Memo is naturally just intelligent, um, he comes across as someone that is quick witted and he's very caring." He explained about the backpack project: "I told them it wasn't for extra credit … and Memo said … I'll get it … and sure enough, the next day he had a toothbrush, toothpaste, and mouthwash or something like that that he went out and bought himself, so I thought that was really cool, that's just the type of person he is though."

Memo's family was on the bare edge of homelessness themselves, but he rode his bike to the store to buy those things.

A small Mexican-style market that used to be right across the street from his apartment had been bulldozed a few years prior, along with all of Glenview's former downtown. More than 50 local businesses and non-profits were replaced with a five-star hotel and office towers that now loomed over Memo's apartment complex. Now, Memo could go to one of two stores. The closer was a Mexican-style market in the Westside suburbs, just a few blocks from Memo's apartment. Memo usually avoided this market, riding further to one that was on the main thoroughfare. It had cheaper prices, but he also felt uncomfortable in some of the white neighborhoods: "It feels weird, I feel like people are starting at me because there aren't really any Mexicans over there." Unbeknownst to Memo, a few years prior, white residents of this neighborhood had protested and attempted to get the Mexican market removed. On local email lists, one resident called Glenview a "disease" and said the market was bringing sickness into the neighborhood, while others talked about calling police on youth who dropped candy wrappers, and many indicated that this kind of market doesn't belong in "our neighborhood." In a community safety meeting, the all-white police force told an overwhelmingly white room of Westside residents that if they had to go through Glenview they should "lock your doors, drive straight through, and don't make eye contact." Memo feeling weird in the space was self-protective. Having the police called because he accidentally dropped a paper or someone decided he was suspicious could have put his life in danger or caused his deportation. He, following his instincts, rode his bike to the far store for the toiletries.

Language in the classroom

Following the community service discussion, Mr Howard rolled the TV cart into the center of the room so students could watch the inauguration while they worked on their essays. He started messing with the channel and the rabbit ear antenna. "See, only the Spanish channel," he lamented to the class and changed the channel. A few of the Spanish-speaking students spoke up:

Memo: Hey leave it!

Other students: "Déjalo!" "Why didn't you leave it?" "Déjalo allí, primo!"

Mr. Howard ignored all of these as he began to mess with the rabbit ears again.

When Memo first came to the US, his mom enrolled him in sixth grade at Dolores Huerta Middle School. Memo's first experiences at Huerta, like those of many recent migrant students in US schools, were awful. "They had me in a class where the teacher didn't speak any Spanish. I had no idea what was going on. I cried every day," Memo recounted. Despite having young children at home, no driver's license, and no education beyond second grade herself, Angelica was able to advocate for Memo—and he advocated for himself. "I called the school," his mother told me. "I told her and she called them," he recounted.

Mexican-American and Latinx families in and beyond California have long histories of educational advocacy and activism. These include everyday advocacy and more systemic struggles against segregation, inequality, neglect, and cultural and linguistic erasure in schools. They have fought for language justice, representative curricula, community respect, and adequate resources (Acuña, 2014; Rosales, 1997). Through lawsuits, protests, and school and pedagogical leadership, families, youth, and educators have pushed back against persistent marginalization and racist policy and practices in K-12 US schools. The defense and maintenance of whiteness has been at the core of segregation and unequal educational policy-making and practice. But, struggles for equity and access often play out within segregated and under-resourced districts, where multiple needs and demands compete for a small piece of the educational pie rather than across neighborhood, district, and school borders, where neighborhood segregation, white flight, and resistance to desegregation continue to ensure educational advantage (Cardinale, Carnoy, and Stein, 1998).

In the Glenview school district, the battles waged by Black educators and families for educational access, sovereignty, and resources did not initially translate into bilingual and English-as-a second-language services. The rapid influx of Latinx families to the district in the 1980s coincided with deep resource deficits, spiking levels of war on drugs and drug-violence induced trauma, and the beginning of backward-progress nationally on desegregation. Local educational leadership was mired in allegations of corruption (which are often targeted at leaders of color in low-resource district in ways that deflect attention from gross intra-district inequalities and racism), and slow to respond to the need for Spanish-speaking educators. Educators worried the extra cost of bilingual services would undermine services for other students in the district and stretch the already tight budgets beyond capacity. While Glenview had a long history of collaborative and expansive racial justice work that included what one student called, the "tri-culture" of Glenview—Black, Latinx, and Pacific-Islander—language policy and practice in the schools stretched these solidarities.

Through his activism and leadership at Huerta, Memo's principal, Mr Flores, worked to address language policy. This became more complex in the wake of the passage of California's anti-bilingual Proposition 227 which banned languages other than English in the classroom (HoSang, 2010). The result of Mr. Flores' advocacy was that, while Memo struggled in his first few weeks at Huerta, his overall experience was positive and supportive. Language advocacy (Memo's own, his mother's, historic legacies of, and his principal and teachers') and a supportive bilingual climate, despite English-only legislative constraints, were key to that success.

Memo's mother stayed active at Glenview Middle School. She took the bus or walked over the freeway and across town with his younger sisters in tow to attend parent education nights, high school information meetings, and other events. These were always bilingual. With a Spanish-speaking principal and vice principal, numerous staff members who spoke Spanish, and a largely migrant parent-body that included a parent leadership team, Spanish speaking families were centered in, rather than peripheral to, or an after-thought of, the school at Huerta. The principal and other key administrators danced and sang during Cinco de Mayo celebrations to the delight of students and families, and English classes and Spanish-language parent groups used the classrooms during after school hours. The same was not true at Westside, where meetings in Spanish were held separately and only a couple administrators and teachers spoke Spanish with any fluency, only one of whom was Latinx. There was, tellingly, no translator at the high school transition meeting at Huerta.

In the inauguration day classroom, as Mr Howard struggled with the rabbit ears, Memo turned and started talking to me in Spanish, insisting that I speak Spanish as well—he was clearly bothered by his language being so overtly dismissed. He'd been working on his essay and already had most of it done. He handed it to me to read. It began, "in my limited experience in the United States, from what I've been able to adjust to, this is a good thing for this country, because it was this country that brought segregation …" The rest of the essay situated Memo as a recent immigrant and drew together pieces of the discussion, before concluding: "I think Obama will help the Mexicans because he's not white and we're not white either." This model of racial solidarity contrasted with the white savior model narrated by Mr Howard. It also made clear that for Memo, as for many students of color in the room, this wasn't about how much had been overcome, but the deep racial inequality that needed to addressed. As I finished reading, the bell rang and we rushed out the door, leaving Mr Howard still struggling with the rabbit ears.

Afterward

Three years later, Memo was chosen as salutatorian and addressed thousands of people assembled at his graduation. He graduated with a 3.8 GPA and multiple awards and scholarships but faced multiple borders as he sought to pursue higher education (Patel, 2013). His family had been displaced the year prior as rent increases pushed them to move to California's Central

Valley. Enduring yet another family separation in the name of his education, Memo stayed behind to finish high school, moving in with his girlfriend's family. Due to the risks of traveling undocumented, and with continuing economic difficulties, Memo's family was unable to attend his graduation. We celebrated with his girlfriend's family in the back yard of her house. We danced and laughed, but the absence of Memo's family cut deep.

Memo planned to start community college after high school. I accompanied him when he went to register. We drove up into the hills and waited in line at the registration desk. When we got to the front, the woman behind the desk began barking questions: "Name?" "Address?" "Social security number?" At this final question both Memo and I froze. We hadn't prepared for what to do. "I don't have one" he said, his voice barely audible. "You don't have one?" she barked back? "No," he replied. "You need one in order to register!" she responded, still projecting throughout the room. Both our faces were red. "Can you please just give us the papers so we can fill them out?" I asked. She shuffled some papers our way. "Next!" She moved on.

Memo's next stop was a meeting with a counselor. He had earned a science scholarship in hopes of studying to be a dentist. We went into the counselor's office. It was a small room with frosted glass walls. "So, what are you planning to study?" the counselor asked. "I want to be a dentist" Memo told him. "You don't want to be a dentist," the counselor replied. "If you wanted to be a dentist, you would have taken four years of advanced science. Look at this transcript. You haven't taken any AP science courses." "I do, I want to be a dentist," Memo replied. The counselor handed him information about four-year transfer requirements and shooed us out of the office.

The community colleges were all long, steep bus, car, or bike rides from Glenview. Without a license, bus or bike was the safest way for Memo to travel. But these options were time consuming. Memo had to work to support himself. He had scholarships to cover some of the school expenses, but he needed to cover travel, housing, and food. Juggling his work and school schedule quickly became untenable. It was 2012 and the Deferred Action for Childhood Arrivals (DACA) executive order had just been issued by Obama following years of organizing by undocumented students and allies (Abrego & Negrón-Gonzales, 2020). As a student, Memo was eligible for two years of protected status. He would be able to get a driver's license and access a work permit but neither he, nor I, was sure if it was safe. What would happen in two years when his protected status wore off? Would he then be on some registry and even more vulnerable to deportation than before? Was it safe to hand over his identity after protecting it for so long?

Memo did apply for DACA but the demands of supporting himself full time, commuting without a car, and his courses proved logistically impossible. He went back and forth between Glenview and the Central Valley working in kitchens and landscaping, the only jobs he could get without papers. Memo did have some success in school and a full-time internship at a local tech company, but his DACA expired and the lack of papers endured as a persistent problem. Memo channeled his intellect into his music, writing under the name The Studier; he interspersed analyses of

Mexican and US politics with narratives of loneliness and loss, playing local clubs and working with a small group of musicians. Listing to Memo's political commentary, I couldn't help but laugh in anger and sadness at Mr Howard's lament that his Glenview students couldn't use an Atlas. Memo was drawing maps of the deep injustices embedded in colonization and ghettoization with his songs, weaving the histories of Mexican politics with those of his communities in California. The fact that he hadn't been taught to use an Atlas at Huerta was an injustice that Mr Howard only saw as a deficit, and the fact that Mr Howard only saw this deficit instead of Memo's knowledge and hunger (of many kinds) was a deeper injustice still.

2
Jaqueline: It's nice but not for us

Jaqueline requested that her pseudonym be Jaqueline. She liked the sound of it. She had silky straight black hair, chunky bright jewelry, and a big smile, and she felt like the name fit her. She was the youngest of four children and the only girl. Her parents had migrated from Michoacán shortly before her oldest brother was born. She had a huge family on her dad's side—he was one of twelve—but her mom had lost all her siblings, one to flu and two murdered, and was now on her own. At her eighth-grade graduation Jaqueline wore, in her words, "one of those dresses that, like, bubbled up from the bottom and it was turquoise, and it had all these little silver sparkles, like, by your waist." She danced on stage as part of the dance team. The packed gymnasium was full of parents, balloons, flowers, leis, candy necklaces, parents, grandparents, and siblings. Families spoke in Spanish, Fijian, Tongan, Samoan, and Indigenous Mayan languages.

Jaqueline's mom and her three brothers were there. Her dad was not. He had been in jail since she was in third grade for domestic abuse. Jaqueline's mom waited until after she started at Huerta to tell her what happened. One day they were walking around a park where they used to go exercise, and her mom said, "I have something to tell you.'" Jaqueline was hurt and confused by the contrast between her beautiful memories and the violence. "He used to pick me up from school. He used to, like, take me out to eat. Everything I used to do with my dad and then all of a sudden he did that to my mom?" But her brothers rallied to support and encourage her: "My brothers always used to tell me, look at us, you don't want to be like us … you want to graduate school and do good." She explained how "I would always cry myself to sleep thinking about it, but then I was like, no, I can't do that for the rest of my life. I mean, I'm going to have to do something and I just thought I should, like, go to school."

University Path

When Jaqueline graduated from Huerta, she applied to a Glenview program called University Path. The program was founded by Shintaira Jones, an organizer with a joyous but serious round face and hair in braids just past her shoulders. On the wall of Ms Jones office was the quote "our deepest fear is that we are powerful beyond measure" with a list of things "we believe in" or "we value" to its side. There was a photo of her son, Marcus, on her desk. She had been a school board member and a teacher and was deeply disappointed at what she saw in both Glenview and Westside schools. When I interviewed Ms Jones, she described her experience getting her son's school schedule when he was transferring into high school: "I go to the schedule and the little line up of classes … I look at it and then I call them up and I say, 'Can you tell me what .5 math is?' … I say, 'Are these courses going to count for college credit?' And she says to me, 'No. Don't you live in Glenview?'… And I said to her, 'do you mean to tell me that my son's schedule is based on where we live?!! Well, I just called to tell you to take my son off the list because my child will never attend a school in your district!'" Ms Jones sent her son to a private school but said, "what happened to my son is the same thing that happens to most kids here." As an advocate, Ms Jones was fierce. She combined high expectations and rigorous pressure with a grounded understanding of the racism and structural obstacles her students faced, not just in general, but in these institutions. This knowledge prepared her to fight for and with her students, helping them anticipate and make sense of what was happening to them (Beauboeuf-Lafontant, 2002).

Ms Jones, like many Black educators, drew on legacies of organizing work, and her own awareness of the risks and costs of that work, in shaping her practice (McKinney de Royston, 2020). "My parents," she explained, "were always involved in things. I was trained that way." When she came to California in the late 1970s, she applied to Glenview School District. They called the next day. "I got a job as a sub at Glenview Middle School and when I started in that class I was their 13th teacher."

Me: That year? …

Ms Jones: Yes! And it was February. I felt so bad for those kids. I told them, I went in there and I'm like, 'You know what, I'm not leaving. … I AM NOT LEAVING.'

She got a long-term sub position and stayed the year. She got angry when teachers scheduled a back to school event and then "bitched because the parents didn't come. They work!!! Come on!!" so she "called the parents and I went to their houses. I got a much better understanding of them when I did that

Me: How so?

Ms Jones: Well, they genuinely cared about their kids' education just like everyone else.

High school: It's full of white people

Jaqueline was mostly enthusiastic about Westside. She liked the diversity and the classes and found most of the teachers were "pretty cool." She particularly liked Ms T, her English teacher, who had one of the rooms where Huerta students seemed to feel most comfortable. I was with the principal one day when he got a call about pink slips (the laying off of teachers). He made sure Ms T was not on the list. "We want to keep her," he told the caller, "she's one of our stars," then turned he to me and said, "we have a new teacher and she's Latina, bilingual, she's teaching our special ed. and our resource classes and she's just done a great job." At lunch Jaqueline and other students often gathered in Ms T's room, eating in small groups or working on the computers.

Teachers of color, particularly Black teachers, were systematically fired in the wake of desegregation amid white refusal to attend Brown and Black schools (Tillman, 2004). The educational pipeline, which excludes many Black and Latinx youth from teacher training (Madkins, 2011; Yosso, 2006), and cultures of whiteness and discrimination in teacher education programs and K-12 schools (Kohli and Pizarro, 2022) have resulted in a teaching force that is almost 80 percent white nationally (NCES, 2020). Most teachers at Huerta and Westside were white, but this manifested differently as leadership of and pressures on the schools were different. Glenview was historically and presently led by people of color and grounded in struggles for educational equity and justice. Glenview teachers' primary responsibility was to Glenview youth and their families. The same was, structurally, not true for Westside.

One early space of struggle for Jaqueline was the bus. The commute was almost an hour long and she was having trouble with a girl who was "mugging her," looking at her in a way that made her uncomfortable. She rode the school bus to Huerta where she could "sit with my friend and we would just sit and wait." The city buses to Westside were crowded with "everyone squishing, you have to stand up and move, people are hella mean." Her mom didn't feel safe with her walking in the dark so on bus days she got up at 5:30 to wait for the bus at her aunt's after her mom went to work. For budgetary reasons (despite their ample resources), the school had never invested in school buses.

The burden of long commutes has persistently fallen on students of color amid white refusal to be bused. Many Glenview students expressed frustration with the buses: they were crowded, often ran late, and caused social stress as students struggled with the uncomfortable physical conditions. As they were often standing room only and packed tight students could not study or sleep during the commute. For a month the buses ran consistently late, but the Westside district counted tardies anyway. The Glenview Catholic priest explained how he and a city council member had gone to the school to fight for the students: "[The city council member] took me to talk to the principal over there … They were glad to see us go! … He took me up there and read them the riot act. You this and you that!" He was raising his hand up and down, pointing his finger as if at somebody, then slamming his fist on the counter. "Well, the principal was saying 'we love these kids and these are some of our favorite kids' and after that was done [the city council member] turned to me and he said, 'what do you think?' and I started in on them with the same thing." Glenview students' access to Westside High School depended, on multiple levels, on the advocacy of leaders and parents from Glenview. Access to Westside's resources had been achieved through years of organizing by Glenview leaders and families and an eventual lawsuit. The work of supporting students didn't stop with access. Glenview leaders, students, and families had engaged in ongoing protest over the years to try and make sure that access was fair, equitable, and meaningful—this was hard and constant work.

Jaqueline did well in her classes, even that first semester. But she wasn't placed where she felt she should have been. The classes her teachers signed off on—AP English and Biology—were different than those she was in, Basic English and Advanced Integrated Science. She attributed this to Huerta's lack of a science program: "at Huerta, we really didn't do a lot of science." She suspected she'd failed her placement test. Huerta teachers and administrators were aware of and frustrated by the lack of a science program. They had heard from the high school that lab sciences were a struggle for Glenview students because they had not previously written lab reports. "Our science program in Glenview is a joke," Mr Flores reflected. He had closed the science lab to try to improve it, but in the meantime there was no lab. He described it as a "double whammy" where students are asked to do something they've never done (lab reports), were not supported, began to fail, decided to drop because they didn't see it as important because it wasn't emphasized in middle school, and then were set up to miss their graduation requirements.

Jaqueline was not in danger of dropping out, but she was systematically shut out of an advanced course she desired, as were all the other Huerta students (such as Memo in the previous chapter).

The fact that there were tracks in the science program at Westside was not simply about the deficiencies of Glenview's science program. It was a result of the systematic resistance to de-tracking from white and wealthy parents. As one of the science teachers explained, the science faculty had tried to completely de-track the science program but when they launched the plan, the former principal "got 200 calls from parents before the school year even started." He explained how one parent had asked "what are we going to do with all these Latino kids?'" But eventually, he said, "the administration gave in to these parents. They wanted Freshman Biology. When the school said they couldn't because it would cost, oh, I don't know, x number of dollars ... the parents just donated that much money to make it happen and then there wasn't any way to resist it." White and wealthy parents in diverse schools frequently shape those schools around their priorities by selectively funding the projects and programs they see as in the best interest of their own children (Posey, 2014).

Jaqueline wasn't just worried about her class placement; she was also uncomfortable with how whiteness functioned, both in and beyond the school. She described the contrast between the middle schools. Of Valley Vista, she said "it's like probably public but it's so full of money and they have everything so it's basically private.... Huerta, on the other hand, is not that good." She knew about Valley Vista because a lot of the students in her Geometry class were from there: "it's full of white people." And while she knew there would be a big white population at Westside, "when you get here, they're like swarming the halls." She knew very few white people prior to coming to Westside. "The only time I ever saw white people," she told me, "is if I did community service … it's hella funny if you see a white person walk through Glenview." I asked why. "Because, you never see it, they stand out so much … there are probably white people who live there too but when you see one it's like, oh my God. The only reason they're there is because of [the new development]." Both the schools and the city were presumably public space, but it was clear to Jaqueline that both functioned through raced and classed practices of producing privatized, privileged enclaves.

Layers of displacement: Gentrification and education

Jaqueline lived in a house in a neighborhood called The Flowers with her mom and her brothers. The neighborhood, full of curvy streets, oak trees, and small homes, backed up against the water and had access to walking trails through the wetlands and marine breezes. White people had left Glenview en masse after the first Black family to move into the area—a professor and a teacher—bought a house in this neighborhood. The all-white neighborhood association had tried to prevent them from buying, then offered them money to leave. When they declined and were backed by the NAACP (National Association for the Advancement of Colored People), one fifth of the neighborhood residents (all white) put their houses on the market.

Real estate agents capitalized on white fear by touring Black people through the neighborhood, posting signs, and going door to door declaring that Blacks were moving in and prices were going to plummet, generating panic selling among white owners. These cheaply sold houses were re-sold to Black buyers willing to pay high prices because there were so few suburbs they had access to—a practice used nationwide called "blockbusting" (Self, 2003). Racial covenants in nearby communities like Westside stipulated "no part of any of said lots or parcels … shall be used or occupied by any person not wholly of the white or Caucasian race," carving out exceptions only so "domestic servants" could reside with their employers. While covenants were declared illegal in 1953, informal mechanisms of exclusion—petitions, real estate steering, and harassment—persisted. A Westside resident remembered a petition circulated to (unsuccessfully) prevent a Black family from moving into the neighborhood as late as 1980. Black buyers in Glenview often had white families stand in for them as fake buyers, among other tactics, to avert racist real estate practices.

These racist housing practices gutted Black economic wealth and the Glenview tax base. White flight combined with high Black demand demographically transformed the city of Glenview in the short span of 20 years. As this occurred, housing demand and access to federally backed credit—which was distributed according to the racial demographics of neighborhoods via a practice called redlining (Rothstein, 2017)—dried up, destroying property values. Property values are the primary source of school funding in most states. As home prices dropped, Black and Brown families not only lost a key source of wealth and savings, an engine that could have funded college educations via home equity, they also lost the tax base to fund schools and basic services. A $20,000 house in Glenview would have to be taxed at a rate of ten percent to raise $2,000 to fund schools. A $200,000 house on the other side of the freeway could be taxed at one percent and raise the same. The tax base destruction was exacerbated as nearby white cities annexed (took for their own) profitable unincorporated parts of Glenview; spaces with industrial bases that could be taxed. The 1971 Serrano v. Priest California Supreme Court decision promised to equalize resources by centralizing and redistributing property tax revenues more equitably. This equalization of tax revenues was undermined, however, by a vote on a bill called Proposition 13 seven years later to cut property taxes statewide and, thus, public school funding. While wealthy parents formed private foundations where they received tax write offs for donating to prop up their schools, parents in Glenview had no such recourse.

Despite the losses of wealth and access to credit for middle-class Black families and of the tax base to sustain social services caused by white flight, population influx continued as Glenview became a safe haven for Black and Brown families amid white racism. Seeing what was happening to schools and services as the tax base declined and crowding increased, Glenview residents organized. A local group of Black, Latinx, and a few remaining white residents began meeting weekly, rotating houses, to generate a plan to take control of Glenview. One aspect of this was incorporation, as the area was not yet formally a city. Organizers didn't just organize on one front, though. Community building and education; local control and desegregation; and local, national, and international work interwove into a networked cluster of projects and initiatives, plans, ideas, and aspirations that began to recreate Glenview as a Black-led, multi-cultural city on the cusp of creative, radical, inclusive, visionary organizing, pedagogy, liberation, and community development. The work included getting community representation on local school boards, setting up an advisory council, establishing a local health clinic, organizing youth teams to help educate younger children and do community education, pursuing multiple desegregation lawsuits, creatively exploring "jump out" and other options in the face of resistance to desegregation, developing local educational programs and independent schools, pursuing fair and just housing options, resisting annexation, addressing police brutality, and supporting community economic development.

By the time Shintaira Jones came to the area, what she described as "a close, tight-knit community, a traditional African American community where the community took responsibility for the kids," was under threat. "Lots of the people … lost everything because of crack cocaine," she said, but she also described how, as a council member and then mayor, she fought, alongside others, for basic resources—Community Development Block Grants, residential treatment funding, redevelopment funding. City leaders worked to get the city the resources and tools it needed, pursuing a range of redevelopment projects. But their success in getting what they needed to develop a tax base that could support schools, police, and services often seemed to threaten the mass displacement of the very residents for whom Glenview had provided some kind of sanctuary. Nationwide and in Glenwood cuts in social services, mass incarceration, and hyper-policing amplified this threat (Smith, 1996). This displacement wasn't just physical, but also entailed a sense that others—those who were white and had more money—were receiving the kinds of basic care and services residents had long desired, needed, fought for, and deserved for themselves.

Many Glenview youth understood that if the spaces they held in this community—homes, streets, schools—were neglected and decrepit, it was despite, not because of, the exacting efforts of their parents and elders. They also understood that these were unstable. Jaqueline explained how she experienced the creation of upper-middle-class enclaves in Glenview as being not just about her and her family's displacement, but about the city "wanting," and caring for, someone other than them. Jaqueline described the houses she saw white people moving into in Glenview.

Jaqueline: They're different than the other houses. They're big and nice and they have two floors. If you go, like, one street away from where it starts, it's so different, it's so perfect and so clean and there's a little park and there's not garbage on the ground and most of the people who live there are white. I guess that's why they keep it that way, because they're white.

Me: How's that?

Jaqueline: Because white people, they get the privilege of people picking up and stuff because they're white and I guess Glenview wants them to stay because they're white and they're brand-new houses and because they get more rent from them.

Me: You think the city wants white people?

Jaqueline: Because you can get more funding so it's probably a good thing but it's not fair because they get whatever.

The houses Jaqueline referenced were those boasted (by gentrifiers) to be "gentrifying" the city—a gated community of brand-new townhouses erected next to the box store that covered the former site of Glenview High School, which burned to the ground in the 1970s. Gentrification is a process of displacement fueled by wealthier, often white, residents moving into poorer, often of color, neighborhoods. Often the neighborhoods have been systemically underfunded by "revanchist" cuts in services, housing, and other social supports. Gentrification is not a simple process of individuals moving but is facilitated by policy through processes like the erosion of tenant protections, targeted development planning that creates semi-private enclaves, and "renewal" programs that demolish existing housing. These are often accompanied by hyper-policing that targets code violations and 'lifestyle' activities such as loud music, littering, or cooking out (Smith, 1996; Lipman, 2011). As articulated by Jaqueline, the border between Glenview and Westside was not a fixed political or geographic boundary, but the unstable line that defined who controlled and benefited from and in space. Residence in Glenview did not entail the same vulnerability for all people (nor did residence in Westside entail the same security for all). White people inside a housing complex designed explicitly to boost the city's tax base through gentrification were afforded private security, private clean-up crews, and private maintenance services in a city where neglect, economic struggle, instability, and dispossession had been normative.

The sense of injustice Jaqueline felt about what was happening in Glenview carried over into how she felt her peers and teachers saw and understood Glenview. I asked her why she thought most kids in her Geometry class were white. "The lower classes have more Latinos and the higher classes are white because their schools prepared them better for stuff. They learn better at Valley Vista because they teach you high and get you ready for higher classes." While, on the one hand, she seemed to be saying the education at Westside High was better than at Huerta, she had strong critiques of her Westside High teachers and appreciated the methods, style, and caring of her Huerta teachers. "It's just Westside is so high and so advanced because they get all these donations from parents, the white kids' parents. The teachers are paid more so it's just harder. It's different. I was used to the way teachers taught us last year. It was so easy to understand them." She compared her math teacher at Westside High, Ms Wilson, to her math teacher at Huerta, Mr Girard. "Ms Wilson's a good teacher, but I only understand her if I'm in the math zone. Girard was fun and he would do activities but here it's all just book work and it's boring and it's really easy to lose your focus because it's boring." Of all her teachers at Westside, she thought only Ms T would fit in in Glenview, "because of her attitude. When she wears her stunners and walks around like she's a model … her attitude is funny and she's hella nice and acts just like us." I asked if it's easier to pay attention. "Yeah, I love her class." The other teachers, she said, are "Westside washed … I just feel like they're like, 'oh my god, my life is so perfect in Westside' and they don't even see that in Glenview it's like, not good, because they're so caught up in their little Barbie land."

Me: Does that make it harder for you to be in their classes?

Jaqueline: It doesn't matter but, like, I feel like they should also know about us too, because when you know your teachers it's really good because it's easier to ask questions. They just know about school and school stuff, but they should know where we come from too.

She contrasted this sense of not being known to her teachers at Glenview. "Your teachers were white there too right?" I asked. "Yeah, they were, but they were more with us. Like Mr Jackson, he was so cool, he would always tell us he hated people who under-graded Glenview. Like I said before, where they come from, people always put us down." I asked if she thought of them as white: "No, I mean, I knew he was, but he would always joke around with us … he was so different. He was so cool and just fun. And Mr Girard, man, I like his funky style. I thought he was cool, and he's such a good math teacher." She felt like the last year, in particular, had been really important:

Jaqueline: I think … they really started to try last year. They really saw the percent of kids from Glenview that didn't finish, and they wanted to start decreasing that percent.

Me: And you think that helped?

Jaqueline: Yeah, because last year they really cared, and they weren't BS-ing at all. The principals were always honest and they always encouraged us. Every day. I mean *every day*.

Me: Do they encourage you here?

Jaqueline: Barely. They do but not a lot.

When Jaqueline started high school, she was aware of how people perceived Glenview and it shaped how she engaged in her classes. She was friends with another Mexican-American student, a girl named Nayeli, who had gone to Valley Vista through the SWAP program but was in University Path with her. When I asked if she was friends with other students from Valley Vista, she started to say yes, but then backpedaled. "In a lot of my classes, it's like, mostly white people, like in Geometry. And well, I don't necessarily talk to them so much because I'm, like, I sort of feel weird because I'm, like, the only Mexican girl in that class. It's me and there's a Mexican guy and there's a Black guy and then everyone else is white. I talk to the Mexican guy because he's right next to me but sometimes I don't talk to the rest that much because, like, I don't always get everything as quick. I don't know what's going on in that class a lot of the time and I feel like all of them, they get it right away, so I feel like maybe they think, I don't know, that I'm not as smart or something but I still talk to them, I mean."

Me: But you don't ask them if you're confused?

Jaqueline: No, I mean, I ask the teacher, sometimes, sometimes I'll ask them, but I feel like, I don' know if it's true, but I feel like maybe they'll judge me. Like they'll just think, what's she doing in this class because she's Mexican and she's from Glenview and even though I'm the same as them. I mean, I belong in the class because they put me there, but I just feel, like, how,

> how you know how they say that, like, they put people from Glenview into lower classes just because they're from Glenview.

This was in January. In April, Jaqueline stayed behind when her mom went to visit her dad in jail so she could go to homecoming. She wore the same dress she wore for graduation. For her quinciñera[1] (her fifteenth birthday party) the next month she was planning to wear white and silver and violet. She'd been practicing her dances. Instead of dancing with her dad, she would dance with each of her three older brothers. She was excited about her little nephew wearing a tux. A change in classroom structure, getting into small groups, had opened up some space to forge relationships with her classmates, and Jaqueline invited a few of the kids from her Geometry class to her quince. The familiarity helped her comfort level, enabling her to more easily check in about the homework, discuss classes, or work through tough problems with peers. She didn't need to be friends with white kids in order to learn—they didn't have any superior purchase on knowledge—but as she described repeatedly, her classes were almost all white so being able to work with these students mattered.

For Jaqueline, one aspect of how relationships with some white classmates mattered was basic support when worried about how to handle the dominant cultures of the school—for instance, the requirement to dress in a particular way for PE, and, particularly, for swimming. This requirement produced a lot of discomfort for students who were conservative in their dress or private about their bodies. Jaqueline struggled with what to do about dressing for swimming. Being able to talk with Cam enabled her to assuage some of her discomfort. Jaqueline described how she "bought, like, the board shorts and a top and it, Cam was like, they told us we were going to swim, and he saw my reaction on my face and he was like 'what's wrong?' and I told him, like 'look!' and he was like, 'don't worry, it'll be fine.' He's so nice!" The change in the seating chart and her outreach to some of her white peers around her quince helped Jaqueline feel slightly less alienated in her classes. But Jaqueline's concern about dress for PE were not hers alone and were not new to the school. They could have been addressed more broadly and long ago with more inclusive PE standards.

Jaqueline's afterward

Ten years later, Jaqueline was working in a skyscraper in the city, having graduated from the University of California. She was still living in Glenview with her mom but now Jaqueline's husband and her one-year-old baby also lived there with them. I had my eight-month-old son with me and we spent much of the time talking babies. I had her draw maps and pictures of the school as we talked and she reminisced. I asked her where she felt comfortable at the high school. She pointed out where she met her husband, the media arts program she enrolled in sophomore year; the space in P wing where "a lot of the Latinos used to sit;" and another area "where, like all, a lot of the Polynesians would be here, and the Black people." When I asked where she felt uncomfortable, she instantly named the grass: "That's where all the white kids hanged out … they would have their little lunch pack … their home meal … [She drew a circle] and then everyone else could, like, be on the outside of it … It made me feel uncomfortable because they would look at us." She described how "you would see a lot of interaction. Not interaction, but like, crossing paths" because there was a classroom close by where a teacher "would have microwaves and she would let us heat up food and a lot of the kids that she helped were, like, the underprivileged kids. Like the low-income kids or Latinos or whatever … I never really had anything happen to me," she explained, "it was just more of, like, knowing that I was not with them. You know. Knowing that they knew I was different and I knew they were different. I had a couple of friends who were white, but we were not best friends."

The other place she identified as uncomfortable was the math wing: "I was always in advanced math, but I was always still the only Mexican girl in my class…like AP Calculus, all the white kids." She talked about how much she hated that class "because of the way [my teacher] would teach. I feel like he'd talk to everyone else besides me." She got a D+ first semester of AP calculus, "and that's when I got really scared because it was senior year and admission to [college] was gonna get revoked." She begged for a C- but to no avail. Her teacher told her not to worry about it, to petition, and that he would write a letter of recommendation. She did write a petition but couldn't bear the thought of petitioning all the schools she had been accepted to. The process changed what school she chose. "The first petition that I sent in and the person got back to me and said I didn't get revoked. So, I was like, 'okay, I'll just stick to that 'cause I'm not gonna struggle, like, I'm not gonna struggle to petition every other school.' I got into, like 20, 18 good schools. I wanted to go to San Diego but once that happened I just never really turned in my paperwork … I got discouraged."

The last place Jaqueline marked was the office of the college counselor, who had accused her of cheating in the college admissions process. "[The college counselor] told me some someone wrote my paper, my personal statement for college, because it was, I didn't have any mistakes. I'm like, okay … " Jaqueline told Shintaira Jones right away. She explained how Ms Jones told her "'that's why we never let our students go with her, because she's always discouraging you guys.'" Jaqueline continued, "That's kind of like an insult. If you're telling me that someone wrote my paper, why don't you tell someone that's white that they wrote their paper? Why? Like, why? It's like all these boundaries and, like, hidden racism and like discrimination and all this stuff. And then [the counselor]'s like, 'oh, I know a couple parents who have done that for their kids.' I'm like, no wonder they get into Berkeley and Stanford and all these crazy schools. And I can't even do that you know!!?? … Shintaira was pissed… she was like, 'don't go to her anymore. Don't go to the college counselor. Take these classes.' And that's what I did." I asked Jaqueline if she could imagine what it would have been like if she hadn't had University Path. "Oh my gosh! I wouldn't've not really known what the requirements were and they would have put me on the basic track and not on a track to go to college, like, that's what happened to my husband." He also went to Westside. She explained how, after they met, he started to wonder how she was doing all of this, preparing for and going to college, but by then it was too late. "Like, you can go to a JC and like transfer, but it's, like, that doesn't sound the same."

Learning objective: Frontiers and borders

The next two chapters, Cam and Amy, raise questions about how whiteness is produced, imagined, and enacted, and what this has to do with (de)segregation, displacement, and dispossession. The lens of the frontier has proved particularly useful to me in shifting my understanding of segregation from one of divided space, where coming together was a solution, to thinking in terms of relations of power. This lens focuses on the dynamics of separateness and togetherness, including occupation, erasure, invasion, appropriation, and exploitation. I moved from thinking about borders, whether as physical separations in space or social dividing lines, to thinking about the power relations lived in and expressed through space. The typical western understanding of the frontier is as the edge of "civilized space," or a line of battle, or an expanse of new possibility. From Indigenous perspectives, the frontier represents an extended site of occupation, genocide, and deep cultural, educational, and social violence (Hurtado, 1988). The colonial ideology of the frontier functions partly by constructing the idea of emptiness or savagery—the imagination of lands open for the taking and minds, people, cultures, knowledge systems, and languages of lesser or no value (Grande, 2018). Importantly, the frontier doesn't just operate through overt physical violence and occupation, but also through the legitimizing notion of spreading or bringing civilization, of improving and educating a lesser other. Education has functioned as a primary mechanism in attempts to erase, replace, and discipline the knowledges, languages, practices, and networks of colonized and occupied peoples, through more or less coercive means. It has also been a cornerstone in being able to define, name, and label those whose lands, resources, and bodies are the object of conquest through their supposed lack of education, knowledge, and civilization. The construct of "benevolent whiteness" and the "white woman's burden" applied to "un-savable people" has functioned as a mechanism for constructing, defining, imagining, categorizing, and remediating "others" (Bauer, 2021). While we might think of the frontier as something from the past, the idea of the frontier is pervasive in both educational work and in the practices and processes surrounding contemporary urban and global displacement (Smith, 1996).

As you read the next two chapters, think about the following three questions. In these chapters:

1) What kind of borders do you see in these (and the previous) chapters? Name as many as you can; include borders that are not physical such as social, political, educational.

2) How do you see these borders being made in these chapters? By whom? Are there ways young people participate in the creation of borders? Who is tasked with crossing or breaking them? In what ways? Are there ways privileges of "movement" across borders is unevenly distributed?

3) How does your understanding of the borders you just identified shift if you think of them as frontiers? Who is displacing, occupying, or subjugating? How are they doing this? What resources—languages, knowledges, relationships, and bodies—are under threat, erased, or threatened with erasure. How? How and under what conditions do people cross these borders?

4) Does shifting from the frame of borders to frontiers shift what you see and how you feel about what you read in these stories? Can you identify borders in your own educational life? What would it mean to think of these as frontiers? What relations of power are present? What is being occupied? Defended? Erased? As you reflect on these, are you participating in occupation or erasure, or in struggling to defend resources, knowledges, spaces, or people? How does this tie to larger historic struggles?

3
Cam: Because she was taking care of me

I met Cam in a High School Algebra class at Valley Vista Middle School. It was my second day on campus, and I wasn't sure where to sit when I walked into the class, so I sat in one of the desks. It turned out I had sat in a student's seat and needed to move. The teacher, Mr Reyes, told me, "It's going to be hard to find a place to sit in here because there's 31 students. If it was a regular class, it would be impossible, but these kids are good." Then he offered me his own seat. A tall white student with curly hair had been trying to sit in Mr Reyes' seat and made a crushed expression as he heard him offer it to me. The couch was unoccupied so I said he could take the chair and I would take the couch. He went to Mr Reyes with the news.

Cam: She said I could take the chair and she'd take the couch.

Mr Reyes: That's not the gentlemanly thing to do. You're supposed to give up the chair for the guest. Sit in your own chair.

He glanced at me writing something in my notebook (it was absolutely unrelated).

Mr Reyes: See, now she's taking notes on you.

I grinned and waved my pen.

Cam: You're taking notes on me? My name's Cam.

I sat on the couch and watched the class. They were doing exam review. The class was all white except a couple of Asian students. The students were ready with questions and fired them off at a pace I found difficult to keep up with: "What is the law of right angles?" "Are those angles congruent?" "How do you draw parallel lines with the compass?"

The construct of the high achieving white kid

Cam was what the Valley Vista guidance counselor would have labeled a "high achieving white kid." When I first talked to the principal of Valley Vista about my project, he sent me to the guidance counselor, Penelope Pruitt, who worked hard to try to figure out which students I might want to ask to participate. I told her I was interested in students who were going to Westside High. She asked me what kind of kids I wanted. and I said I wasn't exactly sure, but that I'd be working with about 10 students. "And how many of those do you want to be at-risk students of color?" She asked. This was her category, not mine, but I didn't want to mess up my relationship with her or fail to understand how she was thinking about this by contesting her language. She continued trying to understand what I needed, asking if I wanted "some high kids and some low kids? I can give you, for example, someone who's likely to really lead the school, someone who's just right at the top, and then I can give you an at-risk student of color." I asked about the possibility of a "student of color who is likely to be tracked high?" She said a couple were going to a charter high school, but she'd try. Then I asked about a "white student who is likely to be tracked low?" Her face twisted a little bit when I said this, and I couldn't read the expression. "I can get you someone," she said.

These ways of categorizing and labeling students are common in schools. Labels such as "at-risk" or "emotionally disturbed," are racialized and classed categories, often automatically combined with "of color". These labels mark failure as characteristics of individuals, rather than situational, structural, and temporally grounded interactions. "High achieving," "smart," and "good," are cultural ideologies, often attached to whiteness and middle-classness that, similarly, mark success as a characteristic of individuals, rather than of systemic social relations (Leonardo and Broderick, 2011). It is common for white educators in particular, even when intending to address inequity, to zero in on students and communities of color as objects of study and critique, or as problems (Love, 2019), rather than critically reflect on how whiteness functions at the individual or institutional level. Educators at Valley Vista persistently assumed I was interested in "at-risk students of color." Over and over again, they told me where I might find these students and what I might see.

Mrs A's room

When I ran into Cam at lunch a few days after we first met, he said I had to visit Mrs A's class. I got there before Cam. When he entered, he came right up to Mrs A, put his arm around her, and started asking her personal questions. Mrs A started joking around with him and a number of other boys. When he saw me, he said "it's you!" then returned to the banter. As Ms A began making announcements to the class, Cam was still standing with his arm around her shoulder. She turned to him and said, "stop hugging me" and removed his arm from her shoulder. He stood for a moment, then put his arm back. "I said, stop hugging me," she reiterated. When he still didn't remove his arm, she said "that's sexual harassment" in a half joking tone, then more forcefully when he touched her again, "don't touch me!" The tone stayed jovial, but Cam's casual disregard for his teacher's instructions and her bodily space were striking. His ongoing negotiation with teachers and persistent disruptions in this and his other classes were treated—as the misbehaviors of white, wealthy young men often are—as youthful, harmless play (McGinley, 2019). Cam readily appropriated the space of the classroom, entered the space of his teachers, and commanded their attention and energy, actions facilitated by his whiteness, wealth, and masculinity.

The tutoring class

One of the other spaces adults at Valley Vista had suggested I visit was Penelope Pruitt's mentoring class, which paired student tutors with tutees. The class was in the Art Room. When I got there, students were waiting outside. Penelope came and opened the door. The students settled into groups of pairs around the large, square, black art tables. Every student in the class was there and each person had a partner. There were a total of twenty-four students. They seemed somewhat awkward with each other and, when they weren't talking about the specific task at hand, the mentees mostly talked to the mentees and the mentors to the mentors. Most tables contained a few students of color and a few white students or Asian students. The students seemed to already know what they were supposed to do. The first thing I heard was Cam talking to his partner. "The things you don't have for this week are …" he said, and he began to list them. His tone sounded tired or exasperated; not mean but maybe slightly condescending, or maybe just awkward at being in that position (I learned later that he was new to this class). His partner's name was Malcolm. Malcolm was Black, tall like Cam, and wearing pants that were faded in the front, dark blue elsewhere. Quickly, Penelope came over to me. "So, what they're doing here is working on filling out their check-in sheet. It's basically a progress sheet where they fill in what they're missing. They do it with their partners every morning and it's just a way for them to check in and see where they're at."

The school had begun the group the year prior. A teacher was paid extra to hold sessions in the morning and afternoon and transportation was provided. "Basically," she said, "these are all the kids who aren't in special education but who need that extra help. What we realized is that if they took their homework home it just wasn't getting done, they would have some story for their parents about how they did it at school or they didn't have any and their parents didn't know any better so they wouldn't make them do it and then they'd fall behind." This way, students had a structured space where they could get homework done at school and not have to worry about it at home. She assured me the program was optional, "only the kids who want to be here are here."

I did a quick count of the pairs. Nine of the pairs were students of color paired with white students. Maybe five or six of the students of color were Black, a few Pacific Islander, and a few Latinx. There were three white-on-white pairs. All the tutors in the room appeared white or Asian. I asked Penelope if the students "ever feel weird or shy about being in here," and she responded in the negative: "No, I don't think so." A couple of students had been doing better and were asked if they wanted to leave but they said no, "that it really helped them to stay organized and to keep track of everything."

The extra space, time, and transportation for supporting student homework is a thoughtful intervention, grounded in communication with students and families and designed to provide material support. It is an intervention that particularly makes sense in a context where many of the students with time and financial resources (primarily white students) were surviving the rigors of the curriculum precisely because of their extensive at-home tutoring support. But the pairing of students in this way, and the inattentiveness to the racial dynamics of this space, also taught the white students to understand or see themselves as superior and, also, as "good." Students did not have the opportunity to consider the circumstances that made it easy, or difficult, for some of them to get their homework in and stay organized, such as tutors, a stay-at-home parents, dedicated workspace, short commutes, and limited outside responsibilities. In this sense, the tutoring class reproduced basic, stereotypical, racialized understandings of students of color as intellectually and academically less capable that many white students already carried.

The Grass

At Westside, Cam hung out on The Grass, the space many students—both students of color and white students who were not part of this group—identified as the most uncomfortable on campus for them. Cam and his big group of friends, all of them white, would sit in a large circle in the patch of grass (the blob described by Ms. Hegel in the introduction, the place Jaqeuline indicated she felt most uncomfortable) between J and H wings, their backpacks all in a pile in the middle of the circle, their bodies packing the space so there was almost no room to pass through. Cam defined his group as the "popular girls" and the guys who hang out with them, adding of the girls "they're nice though, they're really nice." Most of his friends stuck to their own group but Cam saw himself as an exception: "I kind of hang out with everyone." He also hung out with a group he described as "just like really smart people, they're, like, not nerds, they're really smart, they're my friends too."

I asked him "are the popular kids really smart too?" He affirmed "Yeah, they're pretty smart. You know if someone's, like, an idiot." I asked if there were people he didn't think were smart at Valley Vista. "Like some people you knew were like dumb," he replied. "Like, I don't know, it was really obvious because, like, there was a tutoring class last year, like 20 people that might, like, not graduate, like everyone knew who it was. No one really cares though." Cam described the mentoring class as "Sweet … better than homeroom … you can't talk in homeroom … we just, like, checked if they did their homework. Felt good." Cam hadn't seen Malcolm, the student he tutored, since graduation (he went to a different school), but when I asked if he was friends with anyone who was getting tutored he said, "yeah, he was my friend … I'd call everyone my friend." Cam had gained "friends," reaffirmed his own smartness, felt good, and gotten a more fun homeroom through the tutoring program. It wasn't clear what Malcolm got out of having him there. Service-learning projects like this can function as a "pedagogy of whiteness" where racist understandings are reproduced if not directly addressed and interrogated (Mitchell, Donahue, and Young-Law, 2012).

Cam, like most of his peers, didn't hang out with Glenview students. When pressed on why, he raised and dismissed the possibility that it had to do with race. "I wouldn't really say it's racial, 'cause I'm cool with them, it's just they hang out there and we hang out here … Don't really know. Don't really take the time, I guess … they're cool though, like you know them in, like, your PE class …" While Cam identified PE as one of the only spaces of interaction, for him Glenview students seemed to be mostly invisible. "You don't really notice … most people just isolate themselves." This sense of Glenview students' virtual invisibility was consistent with what many other students from Westside told me—it was almost as if they weren't there.

Because she was taking care of me.

Cam came from a large family. They had recently moved and he now had his own room, although he missed sharing with his siblings. His new house was huge. The three-bedroom guest house was bigger than most of the homes of the Glenview students. Cam's father was a leader in a rapidly growing company and his parents donated extensively to the school and the local educational foundation. Cam was a middle child, with siblings both older and younger, and he spoke with only slightly annoyed affection about his family. He was clearly proud of his family and enjoyed spending time with them.

Cam's family employed a full-time nanny from Glenview who had a son Cam's age, Diego, who attended Glenview Middle School, one of the other schools in the Glenview district. I asked Cam about him: "His mom works at my house," he said. "He's pretty cool. He got suspended for punching someone in the face." He giggled. Diego's mom had been coming to Cam's house, taking care of children, laundry, and cleaning since Cam was four. Diego used to come with her but didn't anymore. Cam told me, "He's pretty gangster now … Straight up G…." He said it wasn't weird between them though; they saw each other at school and "It was just like 'what's up Diego and he's like, 'what's up Cam.' That's all we've ever said and then I'm like, 'hey, stay out of trouble.' Some days he just sleeps. I guess it's 'cause his mom's always at my house." "How's that?" I wondered. "I don't know. She just sends him to programs." Cam's words reproduced common white stereotypes that students of color are "bad" and that this is because their parents don't care for them enough (Hagerman, 2018) in the same breath that he recognized Diego's mother's care labor in his own service.

Cam and his family, like many of the families in Westside, were part of what scholars have labeled "global care chains" (Nakano

Glen, 1992) in which migrant women's care is purchased by wealthy, often white, families. Care chains can contribute to radical inequalities in how care labor is relegated and to exploitative labor conditions, even as they may be an important source of income for migrant parents. Patriarchal and racist assumptions about care and motherhood often result in mothers being censured and criticized for not being physically present with their children, this being equated with caring, despite their border crossing and endless labor to provide economically, educationally, and otherwise for their children. Also unrecognized are the myriad ways migrant parents and parents who work in care industries love and care for their children, despite their often very long hours and demanding jobs, including by supporting them economically through their labor (hooks, 1997). Cam recognized there was something unfair in the resources he and Diego had access to, and that one of those things was purchased care. At the same time, Cam's presumption that Diego's mom had neglected Diego in caring for Cam's family was steeped in race and gender ideology. Cam had identified the big structure—the ways he and many of his peers had access to purchased care that somehow came at the expense of Glenview students. But he didn't see most of the broader net of shelters, protections, and advantages that surrounded him, nor the layers and complexities of Diego and his family's life. While Diego and his family had intimate knowledge of Cam's life, Cam had almost no knowledge of theirs. This "racial ignorance" (Cabrera and Corces-Zimmerman, 2017) not accidental and is part of how privilege functions.

Geometry class: Sketchpad

Cam had strong grades, but he downplayed them. "I'd say I'm a good student … sorta … don't do my homework …". He had previously shown me a report card with all A's and A+'s but when I interviewed him mid-year he had two B's. In Geometry he attributed his B to having been caught cheating—sharing his (or his partner's) work. Cam was in the same Geometry class as Khalil and Rahul. There was a computer program called Sketchpad all the students in Geometry were supposed to have. "You don't have to buy it," Cam told me, "but you're F'ed if you don't." They had to do their work on Sketchpad and get it marked off. Cam had done his work with his friend Kelly. He hadn't bought the program, but Kelly had. They worked in a pair. "She has it. I write the definitions." They were only supposed to work as a pair, but Kelly had sent the sketches out to a couple of people who didn't have the software and Cam had sent it to a couple of other people including Khalil. "Khalil just said he was checking it. Checking his work … Stupid Khalil. Actually, Khalil's cool. He's cool."

I had been in the middle of an interview with Cam's math teacher a few days earlier when Cam came by and knocked on the door. He gave Ms Cameron a very long hug which, at some point, she clearly became uncomfortable with. At the end of this hug, after she pulled away, he began to touch and hold her hand and said, "do you want me to tell you a story?"

Ms Cameron: Is it about what we talked about earlier today? What we talked about earlier? The chapter notebook?

Cam:	Oh, I'm not worried about that, it's about that but not about my grade. I don't care about my grade. It's about Kelly.
Mrs Cameron:	Okay, well I'm in a meeting right now.
Cam:	I don't care about my grade but I'm worried about her.
Mrs Cameron:	Okay, we'll make sure we get some time to talk, just not right now.

When I asked Cam about this interaction, he said his parents were less strict and he didn't care about his own grade, so he was trying to take the fall for the cheating episode for Kelly. "My relationship with my mom is fun, I'm just older, she believes I'm more mature, she's like, 'it's your fault' ... just kidding, she didn't really say it's my fault .... Ms Cameron ... called and parents; apparently she, like, she like hinted that it wasn't my fault ... That Ms Cameron was, like, more worried for me than ... something like that." Again, Cam's rule-breaking was minimized, this time by his mother and Ms Cameron—it wasn't his fault, his goodness was intact, and he was treated with concern.

Cam's favorite class at Westside was Mrs White's class. I only visited one time with him. Her class was filled with rich content. They were discussing apartheid and she seemed to be speaking from personal experience and conviction. Despite her content being justice-oriented, she spent a lot of time yelling at students. She seemed to have no inside voice. I managed to walk out of her class feeling embarrassed, angry, and hostile. I took horrible notes because I was so distracted by the dynamics of the classroom. She told me, at full volume, "there are five special ed. kids in here you should work with," and pointed me towards a cluster of students of color on one side of the room. Students of color with learning (dis)abilities often face humiliation and derision in classroom spaces as they interact with the double structures of ableism and racism (Waitoller, 2020). I flushed, mortified at my silence and complicity as students were singled out in this way.

When we got out of class I talked to Cam briefly outside.

Cam: That's, like, my favorite class …her content is really good … and those kids, I mean, they deserve it.

Me: Yeah?

Cam: Yeah, I mean, they're always doing stuff, I mean, like Jeremiah …

Jeremiah's nickname was Jemar. He was a Heurta student and good friends with Rahul and Khalil. Cam trailed off mid-sentence then and left for football practice.

For Cam, his teacher scolding, yelling at, and side-talking to me about other students, who were mostly students of color, was part of what made her a good teacher. Cam loved the content, the critique of apartheid, but did not translate this critique of racist oppression into a critique of the conditions he was living and participating in—conditions some have described as American Apartheid (Massey and Denton, 1993). Cam readily admitted that he, himself, was disruptive in Mrs Cameron's class. Yet, when he assigned blame, in both world studies and in his Geometry class, he assigned it to Black students. Cam was friendly, open, kind, and well liked across the board; Jaqueline and Khalil both spoke highly of him. But he was operating within the frameworks that shaped the underlying logics of the entire school (really the entire nation)—that he and his peers were "good," despite, and even because of, their disruption and delinquency, and others were "troublemakers." White youth are often socialized from a young age to invest in and reproduce the myth that Black bodies are out of control and dangerous; not just deserving of, but needing discipline (Nespor, 1997)

Disproportionalities in discipline where not only completely normalized at Westside High but functioned as part of the discipline structure for white students. At Valley Vista Middle school one day, I found myself in a conversation between the principal and one of the teachers. They were discussing detention. The principal relayed his daughters' experience getting in trouble and having to clean up the school on a Saturday. She came home and said, "dad I'm never going to get a detention, I felt like such a lowlife." The teacher responded, "well, you know if it's on Saturday you've got all those soccer parents watching and they know what's going on … And, you know, you're probably the only person in the bunch who's not a person of color." The space of detention functioned as a space of color, in ways that both reinforced perceptions of Black and Brown criminality and added layers of shame to the rare punishment of white students who, by virtue of their whiteness, were understood as not belonging in spaces of punishment (Cacho, 2012).

It was no secret that many of the white students, including the "popular" ones broke all kinds of school rules and laws, but they were largely protected from juridical consequences. Most of these students, the wealthy ones in particular, had private spaces—houses and vehicles—away from the prying eyes of school and law enforcement officials in which to misbehave. Their suburban streets were not patrolled for threats from within, but from without (Maher, 2004). They had much better protections should they get in trouble: access to parent advocacy backed by threats to withdraw funding (whether in the form of donations or student attendance), lawyers, and funds to enter private recovery programs, pay bail, or switch to a private school.

One seemingly minor but glaring space of inconsistency was dress code. The code prohibited, among other things, "items of a dominant color if gang related" and "shorts or skirts above mid-thigh." Some parts of this dress code were strictly enforced, but the code was flagrantly not enforced for everybody. The "popular" white students regularly violated the shorts and skirt length code with no consequences. Systematic inequalities in dress codes—both in their construction and in their enforcement—contribute to the layered, piled-on, micro-inequalities and indignities students of color, women of color, LGBTQIA+ folks of color (and also white women and LGBTIQIA+ folks, though in different ways) endure in schools (Reddy-Best, 2019; Lewis and Diamond, 2015).

It wasn't just the dress code, but the broader architecture of surveillance that white students were able to evade. Cam's friends partied. Many of them drank and smoked weed, "for sure." They started at the end of eighth grade. Some of the older kids also did other drugs, like cocaine. "Cocaine is stupid," Cam asserted. He said he didn't smoke weed but I asked when his friends did: "Before school? During school? After school?" "Um, all of them, actually," he said, "during, after, actually before. All of them." His friends were still getting good grades. He didn't think teachers could tell: "It's pretty easy to get away with. I'm sure there's people smoking pot on the trail right now." While drug and alcohol use are widespread amongst all youth groups, radical disparities in punishment, treatment, and perception mean the consequences are not (Alexander, 2012).

For the most part, Cam's friends didn't drink at school. After school they'd go to "Julian's house, my house, we just go wherever ... Our junior friends," he said, "they take us wherever we want to go. It was PK's birthday on Saturday. He took ten shots. It was funny." They had been taking shots from a handle of Grey Goose at a Julian's house while his parents were out for a couple hours. His friend had gotten sick and was "barfing everywhere." Then at around 7:00 p.m. "Julian was like 'oh, fuck, my dad's coming' and then everyone just ... that's probably the fastest I've ever run." No one got in trouble. They went up the street and "when his dad passed like us, like 20 of us, he wasn't suspicious ...." When I said 10 shots was a lot, Cam countered, "he's still a lightweight. I took 15 one time ... I threw up everywhere..."

The market for drugs among the Westside students was prolific, and they looked to Glenview students for supply, often in ways that were hurtful to Glenview students. James, an organizer with a local environmental justice group, recalled how, when he went to high school, white students from Westside who he had been to camp with and thought he was friends with barely acknowledged him in high school except to ask if he knew where to buy drugs. Years later, Rahul, who was offered a cheap supply and started selling weed toward the end of his freshman year, described the dynamics of race and class, drugs, and partying on campus: "The white boys' fun is different from ours, you know, like, they go steal bottles from their parents, you know, have little parties at their house … the white boys actually stay in their hood and they party, or like, you know, they go to a family friend or somebody's house, you know, while their parents are out." Parents in Westside often knew the kids drank, sometimes even let them have parties in their homes, presuming that they, like their children, were relatively safe from prosecution.

Drugs were ubiquitous at the school. Rahul explained he sold to "everybody. Everybody that was cool. The white boys, the Asians, the Tongans, Samoans … Black people … the Mexicans and then, you know, all the rich white boys at Westside, they would cash out with me. Like a quarter for like 70 bucks or 100 bucks and shit … They'd be walking around with like Louis Vuitton wallets at like 14 and shit, Gucci wallets and bags and shit, I'm like, I got a Jansport bro … They bust out their wallet and you know you get like four or five white boys all come through with like $50 each and we're over there living off like $10 a day and shit, $5 a day."

In the course of my research, I heard stories of white students doing every kind of drug you can imagine, selling drugs, running from the police, cutting and skipping school, and engaging in all kinds of other illegal and punishable behaviors. I also heard of white parents using drugs and providing their children with alcohol and a place to drink. None of this activity was marked or labeled as criminal. At worst, the perpetrators were considered people with problems, not "problem people"; they were "good kids," "high achieving white kids," not "at risk youth of color."

Cam's afterward

Cam graduated with honors and went to an elite college. He got a job working in the tech industry. I wasn't able to meet with him when I followed up 10 years later, but I heard he was doing well. He is now married, owns a home in the city, and has a steady, well-paying job.

4
Amy: The real world

The student in Mr Howard's World Studies class who was the first to speak during his Inauguration Day discussion (outlined in detail in chapter 1) was Amy Ryan. When Mr Howard called on people, asking what they would take away from that day, she raised her hand quickly and talked about how it was sad Martin Luther King wasn't here to see it. She was sitting in the middle of the section of mostly white students, her back to the door, a few rows up from where Memo and I sat. Amy hung out with the self-described "drama group," a motley group of mostly white students who ate lunch near the art center and defined themselves in opposition to the kids on The Grass. Their group had mostly formed in middle school and merged in high school with a similar group from the other Westside middle school. As Amy described them, "they were sort of the quote unquote 'out crowd' … I don't want to, you know, label us, but we're not the people that would pick on people for fun." She defined her friend group by their kindness and felt that what held them together was "the fact that we have each other's back, pretty much at all times …. It's just such a completely trusting group and it's, if you've got a problem everybody's going to be there to stick up for you."

For Amy, the transition to Westside High had been much calmer than she expected. "I was surprised," she reflected, "at how great it was, honestly … it's really a great school and I'm very, very proud to be a part of it." She felt like it gave her a leg up. "I'm at an advantage over the private school kids because they've been sheltered and they've had their hand held … I'm forced to stand on my own two feet and it's been really good for me." She was getting a 3.5 and on the honor roll. Her classes had gotten switched when they hired in the first week to alleviate overcrowding, but she was mostly still happy with her teachers. She called Ms Fish "the best English teacher ever!" and struggled with her World Studies class just like Jaqueline. "It's very surprising for a lot of us," she said, "because World Studies is, for a lot of my friends it's one of their only regular classes other than PE and they're struggling with it. It's really a very challenging course."

At the same time, for Amy and her friends, Mr Howard's class felt like "almost a completely different world." She explained, "in AS classes people seem like they want to be there instead of 'oh, I have to be at school.'" She felt like students in her regular classes were choosing not to care, in a way that hurt not only them, but her. "There're a lot of people in those classes that just don't want to learn … people will just sort of lay back and not absorb anything and that brings the whole class back." White students and educators often perceive Black and Brown youth as 'not caring' instead of seeing how educational policy and practice have systemically failed to care for them (Valenzuela, 1998). Amy didn't directly refer to students by race or class but she didn't have to; it would become clear from Amy's reflections years later that she was talking about students of color here, but using colorblind

(Bonilla-Silva, 2006) or colormute (Pollock, 2004) language. Despite the vividness of the racial inequalities at Westside, many white students and many white teachers avoided naming or even recognizing race—a means of trying to evade being seen as racist or being accountable for racist structures.

Instead of race, Amy used frameworks like public/private and code words like "gangs" to talk about the differences among students. I asked her to explain how she understood her own and her friends' perceptions about coming to high school. "Um, it's the usual, like ... private school, public school image. Like, all ... most public school people think all private school people are preppy and just are la-ti-da and snooty ... and pretty much all private school people think that public school people are just nasty and poor ... I had this impression that I was going to die my first day of public school." Amy used this public/private framework to talk about her and her peers concerns about Westside, even though Valley Vista was a public school. "Being raised in mostly a private school area and having friends that said, 'oh yeah, Westside's just so bad and they have gangs there and all this stuff and there are drugs going on.'"

Amy was able to make the public/private framework function to talk about Westside by, essentially, expanding the label from an individual school to the entire feeder area. What made this particularly interesting was that Amy had come to Valley Vista from a private school and shared that, at the time, she had many of the same concerns about Valley Vista that she did about Westside as she entered that space. "Oh, when I went to Valley Vista I was, I was scared out of my mind ... I've had that image pumped into my head ... you know, that image of people just being mean and swearing all the time and just being crude, you know, dressing in ripped everything … and I got there and I realized that it was all completely false." Amy didn't manufacture this image, rather politicians and the media have actively conflated Black and Brown, 'urban,' 'public,' and 'youth' in ways that have been highly effective in diminishing support for public schools, social services, and marginalized young people (Soung, 2011).

Amy had a really hard time at private school. She hated it. She had been sick for much of sixth and seventh grade in a way that involved hospitals and surgeries. She switched schools in seventh grade and when I asked why she told me "I was very, very unhappy there … the kids were horrible and teased me about everything and just made everything so much worse."

Me: They teased you about being sick?

Amy: Oh yeah, and it was just a bad environment, it was, you know, I wasn't the lively person I am today.

She had been with the same students since kindergarten but jumped at the chance to transfer to Valley Vista. She felt like they were just "nicer kids … I found a really great group of people at Valley Vista that have saved me in so many different ways." I got to see some of the ways Amy's friends cared for one another and how at least one parent participated in that caring. At lunchtime at Valley Vista Middle, Amy's group of friends hung out at the picnic tables in the center of the quad. Valley Vista had no cafeteria. Students ate outside on picnic tables or the lawn, or in classrooms if it rained. I sat with the group on one warm Autumn day. Amy was there, her thick brown hair midway down her back, as well as two other white students: Annie, who was a little bit jockish and goofy and had her fingers taped from a basketball injury, and Tessa, whose long wavy frizzy blonde hair was held back in a low ponytail. Jenny, who was Asian and also core to their group, was animatedly telling stories. The other girls were in t-shirts and jeans, but Jenny wore a black and white checkered beret tipped sideways on her head, a pink shirt, and pink lipstick. We were sitting in the sun eating lunch when a mom came up to the group. She approached Tessa and said she had read her poem and asked if she was okay.

Tessa: Yeah, I wrote it because I have a lot of friends who feel like they're all alone and I wanted to let them know that they weren't alone.

Mom: So it's about your friend?

Tessa: Oh yeah, it's not about me, it's just kind of about everyone.

Mom: It's a great poem but it's really dark and as a mom I just have to check and make sure you're fine.

Tessa: Yeah, I'm fine.

The mom walked away and Amy turned to me and said, "Tessa's an amazing author. She's written two novels so far and she's working on getting one published." She had written a poem titled "you are not alone" about loneliness and alienation and asked friends to circulate it on the internet. This mom did not know her but had read it and was checking in.

That day, the group was excited about the school play. One of their friends had two parts. The play was called Kokonut High. I went by myself that evening. Next to me was a mom speaking French with her son. A number of people had brought flowers.

The parents were all in casual dress: jeans, vests, designer t-shirts. There was a small group of high school students, presumably older brothers and sisters, and the middle school students who were friends of the people in the play.

The play was about a small island owned by a woman, who was going broke, and the native island inhabitant who worked for her. The island was given to her by the British and now she was threatened by bank and insurance foreclosures. To try to earn the money, she opened a small high school. Drama ensued as mafia and other scammers tried to get ahold of the island. It was a slapstick mystery comedy with lots of hilarity perfect for middle schoolers. The students and their audience had a great time. The text behind this comedy, however, was casually colonial in a way Huerta educators would have been highly attuned to, but that was utterly unproblematic at Valley Vista. The play would have been a powerful opportunity to discuss why and how whiteness became a criterion through which governments stripped people of land and gifted it to others. It could have produced conversations about what it meant to endeavor to hold onto stolen land, about settler colonial occupation, and about labor relations amid occupation (Tuck and Yang, 2012). Or it could have been about educational inequality and what it meant that these students could get credentials just because they could pay. But neither the play nor its production was intended to critique any of these. The play took for granted the colonial context, using it merely as a backdrop, not as a site of interrogation.

In the classroom as well, it was easy to see how frameworks that would have been critiqued at Huerta—not just by faculty, but by students as well—pervaded. The English classes had been working on biographies. In contrast to Huerta and many of the lower track freshman English classes at Westside, where this standard was met through "I Have a Dream Speeches" focused on social change, the biographies at Valley Vista largely centered individual success. I had observed Ms Hegel's class a few days prior. Ms Hegel was a young white woman with long, thin, dark brown hair. She wore a lot of jewelry: bangles on both wrists, necklaces that draped around her neck a couple times. The classroom was set up with desks in rows facing the front. I sat in a squishy chair off to the side by the door. Class was focused on making thesis statements more detailed and specific: "Right now you might have something like, 'X worked hard and made himself a success.' What I want you to do now is make it so that your thesis explains why that was important to your subject, why did it matter that he worked hard and made himself a success? How did he work hard?" She had students work in groups, sharing their thesis statements with each other. Then she read and corrected some examples from the group. Most of the examples were, unsurprisingly, about people who worked hard and became a success. This "myth of meritocracy"—the idea that hard work results in positive outcomes—sustains the idea of equal opportunity even in the face of glaringly inequitable systems (Ladson-Billings and Tate, 1995)

The school offered the students no tools to think about how success might be shaped by anything besides individual effort. The educators were well aware of the privilege of many of the students. Many of them were children of CEOs and inventors, heirs to fortunes. Ms Hegel described students' surety about their future security as a source of motivation but worried "it could almost be detrimental because they have so much support and tutor support and stuff you wonder if they're really ... being able to find out who they are as a student." But then she said, "it's weird, because I feel like we have such a spectrum," continuing, "we also have the kids that are bused in that come from the total opposite side and then we have kids who have, you know, a different tutor every day for a single subject."

Despite this clear acknowledgement of dramatically inequitable academic resources (private tutoring, financial security), Ms Hegel did not name ways that this might undermine or contradict the hard work, no excuses narrative. Rather, she attributed inequalities to culture, stigma, natural ability, or knowledge. She described how, out of 50 students she has in an average year, there are "probably 10 or so that throughout the year have issues with grades." Of these, she said "I would say maybe only three or four of them are because they truly don't have the natural ability and they need the support...the others are just laziness or motivation or, you know, self-destruction." Ideas about "natural intelligence" are systematically racialized in the US; the pseudo-science of race shaped the construction of supposedly neutral measurements like IQ (Gould, 1996). Ms Hegel had few SWAP Program students—"I probably maybe have three or four each year"—but it turned out these were the students whose ability she doubted: "in truth, I mean, sometimes they are the same students who really struggle and probably just because of ... always having that kind of stigma or maybe it's because of a true, I mean, you never know why." She went on to talk about how some SWAP Program kids do fine, but wondered if their struggles might be because they "don't have that same worldly knowledge... so many of these Westside kids... they've traveled the world by the age of, you know, 14." "It's sad," she continued "but I feel like transfer kids end up being their own clique." She did not discuss whether the abundance of tutors, her own pedagogy, or the culture of the school might have some role in marginalizing SWAP students.

In describing what this "worldly knowledge" looked like, she said, "some of these kids ... they just have like everything at their fingertips ... I have kids who do fencing, I have kids who travel 40 miles for dance ... anything they have an interest in ... they're so over-programmed with stuff. A lot of my kids will talk about spending x, y, and z at their summer home or their home in Tahoe." During Christmas break she "had a kid going to Tahiti, I had two going over to Europe, I had, like, five going to Mexico, like seven going to Hawaii ... It's really insane what they have and what they're exposed to and what they can do." She described her students as "angels," comparing them to students she'd seen on field trips from other schools "in public museums ... screeching and running and breaking stuff," saying, "you forget what the real world can give you." She didn't feel her students lived in the "real world" but that didn't stop her (and others) from holding the products of their heavily subsidized educations and lives, made possible by seemingly endless resources, opportunities, and support as the standard everyone else was expected to meet. This excess wasn't seen as cheating, but as knowledge, as "hard work".

I asked her whether they had "some type of multicultural curriculum" at the school. She talked about how they were doing a "walking in their moccasins" program, "looking at things from somebody else's point of view and thinking about it, walking in their skin, walking in their shoes, walking in their moccasins." She explained how she tried to choose read-aloud books that "fit into that spectrum, whether it's a kid looking at the time of the Second World War or during the Depression or a quirky girl in high school or, you know, *To Kill a Mockingbird*." She felt like this had some sort of impact: "These kids can say some really insightful things ... they write in their grad speeches about, you know, going to Cambodia and seeing, oh, how poor these kids were and they can't imagine how much a dollar means and they find dollars in their pockets ... so I feel like they do get it." "Get it" here seemed to refer to recognizing their own privilege , but hinted at no real knowledge of Cambodian people and histories—Cambodia became a "poor" backdrop against which young tourists could understand themselves as "lucky." She also justified her students' broader lack of critical engagement with inequality "you have to step back and be like, okay, this is what they're supposed to be like at this age ... most of them are not mentally ready to be worried about, you know, a family that can't pay for food that week, when they're worried about getting an A on a test ... they just can't balance that." Of course, many Glenview families and students were very worried about how to pay for food and Glenview students often had to balance these things in order to survive or thrive academically. While Ms Hegel described herself as a "no excuses" teacher, the rigor of her curriculum seemed to stop at the point where her white and wealthy students would be compelled to critically reflect on their own privilege or question their own knowledge and frameworks.

"Worldly knowledge," as Ms Hegel talked about it here, was something conferred not by complexity of experience, diversity of deep relationships, migration, or perseverance in the face of layered obstacles, but by privilege, by having everything at your fingertips. Contemporary US understandings of knowledge and education are tightly tied to coloniality—to processes of conquering, collecting, and categorizing. Indigenous knowledge does not become knowledge until written about by white explorers (Willinsky, 1998). The idea of walking in someone's moccasins is an appropriation that allows students to "play Indian" without interrogating their presence on stolen land or in stolen shoes (Tuck and Yang, 2012). This mildly "multicultural" curriculum read much like the students' "worldly knowledge": as a series of sheltered trips to other places that would allow for superficial knowledge and performative sympathy without real engagement or serious interrogation. I was reminded of James Baldwin's (1984) warning of the "ignorance" and "power" that come from investing in whiteness and "opting for safety instead of life" (pp. 179).

A lot of what Amy talked about, in terms of what mattered to her in and beyond the transition to high school, was her expanding understanding of the world around her. In January, the school hosted an event called Dialogue Day that was designed to build community amid diversity. It was an expensive, contracted, school-wide event, led by professional facilitators and recommended by Oprah. The event included exercises to challenge students to reflect on their privilege, position, and experiences, such as walk the line, and sharing in groups of five where they were asked to address questions about their experiences. Each group had an adult present who was briefly trained to report back to counseling services if they thought anything needed attention. Responses from students I talked to about the day ranged from apathetic to enthusiastic. Amy was enthusiastic: "What happened at Dialogue Day was completely a surprise … the ability to just let that go, let all that stress out was just incredible to me." She also felt she had learned a lot about her friends, saying, "I thought I knew my friend … she was always the really happy person and she's always really fun … turns out she's [been through a lot]… I just learned so much about her … It's been life changing this year."

Amy described her own family as "tight knit." They lived in a large gated house on a quarter acre of land in Westside. She had lived there since she was six. Her dad grew apples and roses and vegetables in the yard. She described how she and her mom drove by one day while the house was being built "and we pulled over and I remember saying to my mom 'what are you looking at?'… she said, "I think that's gonna be our house." Amy was "extraordinarily close" to her mom: "She's my best friend … I just feel like she's, my family's always gonna be there for me, they're always, like, my parachute." Her confidence had been shaken recently when her grandma had died and her mom's side of the family "completely fell apart." A relative had accused her mother of abusing pain medication and they had fought over inheritance; "it was really, really tough for about a year and a half."

By April, Amy had a boyfriend. "He's cute, he has curly hair," she told me. I'd never met him but she said they'd been dating for six months. There was construction going on at the school, so Amy's group of friends had been sort of wandering the school trying to find a new eating place. She was already planning her classes for next year. She was going to take AS English II and Western Civilizations, which was an advanced but not AP course, and was planning to go to summer school so she could jump a level in math. Her seventh-grade test scores in math and science were high, but because she took middle school Algebra she wasn't placed into Geometry and couldn't get onto the honors track in science without Algebra II. The high school, due to budget cuts, wasn't offering summer school to students who weren't failing, so Amy was taking summer school at a private school. "I can … be in an environment where people aren't failing which is nice, very nice." The class would cost about $500, a small sum for Amy's family but a months' rent for some of her peers.

Amy didn't drink. Mostly when her friends got together they would "do a movie night or … eat a full carton of ice cream and energy drinks." Her dad was a wine collector and he "lets me have a sip sometimes and on really special occasions he'll let me have a small glass because my parents have this theory that if I don't get used to it now then in college I'll go insane." She felt like she had "doubled or tripled" the number of friends she had during the year, but they were all from Westside schools. Even so, she felt like he had grown from being "completely innocent" and "afraid of new things." I asked what she meant: "I wasn't used to that. I wasn't used to a lot of the hard realities of the world, like how some people really can't afford to buy a home computer … or to go and get a lacrosse jacket that's $95." She described one friend who was struggling with money because her parents were divorced and another whose "dad got laid off, so they're living off of savings." "People in classes," she went on, "will be like, oh, yeah, I couldn't come to homecoming because I couldn't afford it, or I couldn't get there."

Amy's afterward

While, by the end of her freshman year, Amy was still largely hanging out with Westside students, when I met with her 10 years later, she described how this had shifted in the later years. She had helped form a school choir with her music teacher that included many Glenview students "because it was an elective that didn't require any extra, like, money … and a lot of people had done stuff with their church and knew how to sing that way." For Amy, "it was really one of the first places at Westside that … everybody was on a level playing field. It wasn't like people who lived in mansions in Westside were any better or any more deserving than people who lived in apartments in Glenview." She became invested in building community: "My teacher and I would try to get everyone together and try to break down a bunch of barriers." In her first class, Amy remembered being "absolutely terrified because I knew one person and, kind of, the Glenview kids have, sometimes have a rough exterior" but then around Thanksgiving they were talking about different traditions and "something somebody said just totally shocked me, like, 'oh, we can't, you know, afford a turkey in my family' and I was like, 'what?!'" That comment pushed her to "realize that something wasn't quite the same there." Sometime after that, as she recounts it, she approached a Glenview student and said "'I think we're going to be friends'… and that was kind of when everything, people started opening up." They began talk about families, how "people had two jobs and that's why they couldn't get their homework done on time or they couldn't go to after-school events because they had to pick up their younger sister or brother because their mom was at work or they couldn't get to the event that we were doing because the bus didn't run or whatever." In short, Amy began to learn about how structural inequality shaped the everyday schooling she had assumed was fair.

As Amy started to see the inequality more clearly, she began distancing from her old friends: "They'd say like, 'oh no, I understand, I have struggles too. I understand.' And it's like 'you're not getting it, you're not getting that there are so many people who can't even afford books or can't afford whatever and here you're complaining about the fact that you aren't getting a car on your 16th.'" When we returned to the question of the transition to high school, she reflected, "it seems like that would be a big transition but it wasn't, it was a continuation of what I had been doing … it wasn't until I got into choir that I realized that there was anything different and that caused tension."

I asked Amy to draw the school and to talk about social groups, race, and her own comfort in relation to her map. She said there were places she felt really comfortable, like the choir room, but her friends didn't, and so, when she was with them, she felt uncomfortable. "Or if I went around people who were … of different race and background, it was out of place because mostly because my friends were, like, 'you're not supposed to go over there.'"

Me: Yeah? Did folks talk about it?

Amy: Oh my God, yeah.

Me: How would they talk about that?

Amy: Carefully.

Me: How so?

Amy: They would really try to be politically correct, which is funny because we were talking about race and we were being racist which I was very aware of. Or trying to be aware of in high school, I guess. So it'd be like, well the, you know, you don't wanna go over there because, you know, Crips are over there, and it'd just be … I didn't even know what that was when I got to high school … we were trying to define race but didn't want to say that because it wasn't cool to say that. Like it wasn't okay to say that.

The last time Amy and I talked I asked about her dropping a level in English during her senior year. She critiqued her teacher and then I asked if the students in that class were different and how.

Amy: Almost entirely, like, African American and Latino.

Me: What was that experience like for you when first went in there?

Amy: It was frustrating, and it was annoying, because the culture of the class was not to care. It wasn't like, appreciative of … it was all about getting out of class and skipping class time … I wasn't friends with anybody there.

She described a day when the whole class skipped together but she didn't: I was the only person in class." She did make friends but "it took … a long time and then second semester I was in a different class. It was, like, a different expectation. It was really, it made me feel dumb … I went from expecting you to understand to expecting you not to understand anything, so it was just, we'd go to class and they were explaining line by line one chapter of one thing and I was like, no, I got that." Amy was frustrated with the class but rather than attribute her peers apparent "not caring" to the deadening and demeaning curriculum and struggling teacher she described—she seemed to imply they lacked appreciation; a common critique levied at students of color exercising various forms of "critical citizenship" (El-Haj, 2006), including refusal to participate, in degrading or inequitable spaces or under unjust conditions.

Amy had done an internship in Glenview during college, so we talked about her impressions both before and after this experience. She had only been into Glenview once during high school, to drop a choir friend off at University Path. "I just never went over for anything and you went over the bridge and it was an entirely different world and I remember getting off at that exit and being shocked at the fact that there were like gates up and ... downtrodden houses and they were half a mile away from where I lived and I'd never really experienced that. I felt very protected and naïve." She could see inequality, but that wasn't the same as seeing the labor and love that Glenview residents had poured into the city and one another, the knowledges residents carried, nor the ways her own communities had contributed the conditions she witnessed.

Amy, like Cam, had a nanny from Glenview. She was Fijian. She took Amy to her apartment once when she was a kid and "told me never to go over there, but it never really clicked until I went over there myself and I was, like, shocked. It was this whole new world. I remember my parents talking about Glenview and shootings

… my friends that lived in Glenview and … saying that that's a rough area, but I don't think they ever told me outright not to go." This is what Westside young people (and many adults, including the teachers) knew of Glenview and thus, when Glenview wasn't invisible to them, it became visible as a space of threat, violence, and lack.

The clinic Amy worked at had been founded by a community organizer in the 1970s from Glenview who sought grant funds to open a space that could serve the community. It was part of a broad slate of organizing efforts that sought to secure services for the community and was run by and for Glenview residents. The leadership was almost entirely of color and many of the staff were local. Amy had gotten an internship working on a grant, surveying people about their dental care practices and seeking funding. While Amy had begun to think about Glenview in a more comprehensive way than when she was younger, she still largely framed herself in a helper role, still largely talked about people from Glenview through this lens, and was still nervous and scared in the city. She found herself relying on Glenview residents and staff and her classmates to help her try to learn what her high school had not taught her (although she learned some in choir): how to treat people from Glenview with decency, care, and respect, to honor their work, and to value their time and expertise, and be humble about her own.

Amy told me her internship had been really "eye opening." Her job was to write a grant to get extra funds to help get access to dental care and dental education for families. "It was just," she told me, "a really interesting process to get to focus on something so simple as teeth, which isn't simple at all, and learning how Glenview and over-the-freeway functions, it was like two totally different worlds." She was surprised by the barriers to accessing dental care and the everyday ways tooth pain and decay affected children and family's lives. She had interviewed and photographed patients, "and I got to know some of the staff because 40 or 30 percent of the staff was from the local community and you'd go to their board meetings and you'd get to know all the fundraising people and the people with the money."

Amy told me she had learned about privilege. I asked her what that meant for her and she told me a story. She felt like her Glenview Health Clinic badge operated as a form of protection when she was in Glenview: "You're here to help so we're going to be, do everything we can to be nice to you since you're helping us." She described one time when she had to run back and forth between buildings to copy forms. She was in dress clothes, in 90° heat. First, "this lady came up to me and she said, she gave me like this lecture about how I needed to slow down, nothing was that important." Later, as she continued to go back and forth, some men had been cat-calling her and "one of the guys from the clinic who I didn't, I had met him once, he came up to me and said, 'you're just going to keep on walking with me and I'm going to walk on by you and it's going to be okay.' She was shocked by the casual way that he took care of her, "I had never really experienced that before and to just have it be so normal, just like, I'm going to walk you and it's totally just, I've never met you but you're out of place and you need some help … it was a guy and a girl … and it was the nicest thing that they could have done … but it was such a reality for them." Whiteness no doubt shapes this encounter. Amy saw herself and was likely seen as extra vulnerable and got extra protection because of her whiteness. But she also got a glimpse of the everyday ways many Glenview residents take care of one another (extended, in this moment, to her), so startling to her because of its presumed lack.

Amy had done this internship as part of her studies at a liberal arts university on the East Coast. When we met and talked, she was post-graduation and looking for a job. She wanted to work in health care or philanthropy, and she wanted to do "big impact," not just "boots on the ground" work. Despite her deeper understanding of inequality, she persisted in a frame of "benevolent whiteness" where she and her community were valuable helpers (Applebaum, 2010). She had thought about working in other places but realized "the big honey pot for funding right now is here and I know people and my dad knows people and my uncle knows people here so all these connections and, um, I couldn't just ignore that. I mean, the impact I could have once I get a job, I mean the impact I have could be huge because I'm already in those networks … I went to school with the founder of [Major Tech Corporation]'s kids, you know, that kind of stuff that I had, I hadn't even paid attention to and then all of a sudden that's the reason that I'm such an asset now." Amy's connections to wealth, which, because of systemic segregation, were not shared by her peers from Glenwood (who had much deeper knowledge of and connections to the city), now put Amy in a position to "help," a position Amy hoped to leverage to secure not only resources for the clinic, but also a job for herself.

Learning Objective 3: (De)segregation

Often, understandings of segregation mistakenly emphasize space, physical separation, or separateness. Segregation is none of these alone. Rather, it is a relation of power. It is a form of subjugation imposed by a dominant group, through the state or extra-state means, that is designed or functions to prevent equitable access to full citizenship, belonging, participation, and rights. It is structured to humiliate, degrade, and mark those who are segregated as contaminated or inferior.

When marginalized people self-isolate for their own protection against violence from dominant groups, this is not self-segregation. And when people design learning spaces and institutions to emphasize histories, visions, and points of view that have been excluded by dominant institutions, this is also not segregation. However, when people in dominant groups draw upon racial power or privilege to create spaces that are racially marked and coded in ways that produce hostility, harm, discomfort, and oppression such that subordinated groups are excluded from basic rights, privileges, resources, and access, including the right to participate or be present, this is segregation. Segregation does not have to be overt, state-sponsored, or fully exclusive. But segregation is not mere separation; it is a hierarchical spatial arrangement marked by relations of power.

As you read the next two chapters, think about the following three questions. In these chapters:

1) How do the young people and educators in these chapters talk about segregation and desegregation? What are some

examples of what these seem to mean to different people at different moments?

2) If you think about segregation as a relation of power and domination, what examples of actual segregation do you see in these chapters? What makes you call the examples you choose "segregation"?

3) In what ways do the young people or educators in these chapters work to challenge or contest segregation? From your perspective what, if anything, do these actions have to do with educational justice and rights?

4) In what ways do you see segregation and desegregation affecting the students' educational experiences?" How do these compare to your experience?

5
Khalil: They played me

I met Khalil when he was in eighth grade at Dolores Huerta Middle School, in Algebra class. His teacher asked for volunteers to solve an equation and his hand quickly popped up. He was seated at the back of the class, his hair arranged in precise cornrows that wrapped around the contours of his head and extended an inch or so down the back of his neck. He strode confidently to the front and started working the problem on the overhead projector. Students were sitting in rows of four, facing away from the doors of the classroom; the room was slightly dark so the projector could be seen, the long Venetian blinds pulled shut but with light leaking through wherever slats were missing. He stood at the projector, working on it for a minute before his teacher intervened: "Looks like you don't quite have this one," the teacher said, and showed the class the problem. What struck me about the interaction was Khalil's confidence. While he had gotten the problem wrong, his interaction with his teacher was easy and familiar. He went back to his seat and studiously watched the teacher, taking notes and revising the problem in front of him. I had the sense he was a student who usually gets the answer right. I was right: he was a top student.

Khalil had spent much of the previous few years homeless, living out of hotels, shelters, on friends and relatives' floors, and in his mom's car. By the time Khalil entered eighth grade, he and his mom and sister were living in their own apartment on the west side of Glenview. It had a big fluffy couch that Khalil and his sister fought one another to sleep on (despite having their own beds), and there were diplomas and family photos all over the walls. Khalil's mom, Camila, had worked two jobs and saved for months to be able to make the deposit on this one bedroom. "At that time, the rent was really reasonable," she remembered. She planned to live here briefly then move on, but rents had been rising, fueled by a "predatory equity scheme" being waged by Wood's Edge Properties. This investment group had bought almost all the Glenview properties on the west side of the freeway around the time Camila moved in. Then they immediately sued the city, contesting Glenview's rent control ordinance. Eventually they won, overriding the ordinance and costing the city millions in legal fees. With rent protections gone, the corporation raised rents $300 in a single month. They also all but disappeared from the daily lives of residents as managers of the building. The city had fought three battles with the owners in the past five years, trying to keep rents down and demand maintenance. It was widely believed, however, that Wood's Edge Properties was aggressively trying to drive residents out to facilitate a process of condo-conversion—a change that would likely "flip" these properties from low-income residents of color to high and middle-income mostly white residents like the surrounding communities.

Camila and her neighbors had complained and protested: "it's been crazy, we've been to city hall … I had my two minutes to say what I had to say." She was concerned about the rent increases both displacing her, and making it impossible for her to move. She wanted to move, but she did not want to be back on the streets with her children. She wanted more room and more safety, but she also explained that she wanted to stay in the area because of the schools: "I want them to continue to go to Westside High because I think that was the best since we've been here." Not only did she like the quality of the education, but she also didn't want her kids to have to change schools again. The ability to stay in one place mattered. Reflecting later on why he loved Huerta Middle School so much, Khalil said, "I think it was the first time I got to stay at a school longer than a year and a half or something, 'cause I went to a lot of schools so I think that's the only thing I liked, that I got to keep my friends for more than a year and a half." With that stability, Khalil's sister Shayla had gotten involved with a community mural project, Art Wall Program, exploring the history of Glenview and drawing herself into it. Through that work she had learned "all about aspects of art in the community and trying to make the community better, as far as Glenview." Camila talked proudly of the mural Shayla had worked on, "the big mural outside of Huerta … Shayla's on that wall. She's actually out there on that wall."

At Huerta, Khalil was a star player on the basketball team. He hung out mostly with Rahul, who had been his best friend since he came to Huerta in fifth grade, and his friends Jemar, Malik, and Tiny. At lunch I could find him sitting in the grass, wrestling, laughing, talking with friends, shooting baskets, or in classrooms studying. When I interviewed him during his eighth-grade year, they had just lost their championship game against the all-star team, but he was proud of their season. Mr Jackson, Khalil's basketball coach, was one of his favorite teachers at Huerta, although his all-time favorite teacher had been the only Black teacher he had ever had, Mr Green. When I asked what made Mr Green so good, he said, "I don't know, he was just so calm. Like he has so much authority, not to be yelling. Like, teachers usually gotta yell to get authority. He'd never yell, like to get it, we just respected him a lot. He'd never yell at us. He was just a calm teacher. I think when the teacher's calm the students are more calm." Mr Green had left Huerta to go back to school. The four eighth grade core teachers that year were all white men, most of whom had little, if any, teaching experience prior to coming to Huerta. Mr Jackson was one of the most prepared. He had wanted to be a teacher since junior high school, gone through a full teacher training program, and taught in an elementary school he described as "almost identical" to Huerta in Denver. He was in his fifth year of teaching.

Mr Jackson's eighth grade language arts classroom was the first class I visited at Huerta. Khalil was in there, but I didn't know him yet and didn't notice him. I had just sat down and gotten myself nervously settled on the edge of his room when I saw Mr Jackson don an enormous, WWII style full face gas mask and open the door to greet the students lined up outside. I noticed, in this moment, that he was also wearing a t-shirt with a picture of himself holding a giant fish on it. The student's came in talking loudly and laughing. "I'm sure you noticed," he said in a booming voice as they entered, "the smell!" Students were listening and continuing to giggle as they took their seats. "I'm wearing this gas mask in solidarity with the smell!" The fish tank had broken, and they had shampooed the carpet the night prior, but the room still smelled. "But are we going to complain about it??!! No! What do we do with problems? We make them into opportunities!!!" Mr Jackson set the students up for a free write on the smell. They wrote without making a peep for seven minutes, then Mr Jackson asked for volunteers to read. One was about how an animal took "a big, hairy, brown dump" in the corner, another about Mr Jackson's feet, and a third about "someone's giant pimple they popped." Mr Jackson reacted as they were read–disgust, amusement, awe. He repeated small pieces of each story and said "that's a really vivid description. I can really smell it when you say it like that. Gross!"

The class spent the rest of the day in the computer lab working on their I Have a Dream speeches. Before we went in, Mr Jackson checked in about student's different abilities and spoke about how to care for the technology: "Don't knock the computers. It's really important. Those flat screens are really expensive." Typing abilities varied—"how many of you hunt and peck?"—as did how far along they were—"some of you will need to pick up the pace." Students from Mr Jackson's class would be spread across all five tracks at Westside. The differences many Westside teachers lamented, Mr Jackson embraced.

When they got to the computer lab, some students were stuck on where to begin. "You want to begin by talking about the problem" This is an I have a dream speech so you're writing about something that you want to see changed. He called on a student:

Mr Jackson: What's your dream?

Student: That everyone should graduate high school.

Mr Jackson: Okay, that everyone should graduate. That's a great dream. So, what is the problem that people aren't graduating? Are there some numbers that you could use? What percent of the kids from this school graduate high school?

Student: Eleven percent?

Mr Jackson: Eleven percent, that's right. Eleven percent. So that's a problem. What percent of the students are eligible for college? Six percent. So those are some really powerful numbers that you can start off with.

Mr Jackson was ready with information about the conditions his students were experiencing to help students ground their work and analyses.

I talked to Mr Jackson after that first class and he asked me what I thought with evident pride in his voice.

Me: These guys seem great.

Mr Jackson: They are, they get along, they take care of each other.

This aspect of taking care of one another was a lot of what Khalil reflected on years later about his time at Huerta. "I honestly," he told me, "think Huerta was like the best years I've ever had. I mean … everybody was cool at Huerta. I hated high school." I asked him what made Huerta so cool; "I don't know. Everybody knew each other. We came back the next year. Everybody was cool … There were, like, not that many secrets. I don't know. You knew everybody. I liked that you knew everybody I guess."

This sense of community wasn't accidental. Mr Flores had worked really hard to cultivate a sense of care and community at Huerta. Mr Flores described how his own practice came in part from watching his grandfather. His mother and his uncle both had prominent positions in a mayor's office of a nearby city and his grandfather, this "old Mexican dude," an immigrant with a third-grade education, worked as a janitor in that same building. When his grandfather would tell people this, "people would start laughing. What? Your whole family's running this joint, I mean, and you're the janitor, okay." He explained how this led him to, as an RA at the nearby university, "want to teach my residents to connect … most of the people working there were from Glenview so I got to know most of their names and I would model that for my residents … 'you need to know Lucy, you know, Lucy's really cool' … You need to know these people and you need to speak with them." Mr Flores built on these understandings of relationship building as he studied both pedagogical best practices and the history of Glenview. He drew on a knowledge base housed in centers and research units built through movements for ethnic studies and racial justice and generated by former university students with deep relationships with Glenview. He also began, early on, working with Glenview youth, elders, and community members.

This sense of care and community was what many educators, including Mr Flores, worried was completely lost with the transition to high school. "Glenview, it's like, everyone's in one city and then they go out to completely different municipalities where there's basically just no relationship with them … zero. And, like, the kids don't even know where the hell the schools are …. So, it's like, desegregation policies have, I don't think the potential benefits of putting some student, sitting next to a white kid, is outweighed by the adverse impact of, like, making you leave your community and work with people who really have no vested interest in the success of your community …. You know people in [these surrounding communities] really could care less about Glenview. I mean, they might in the sense of 'oh I, you know, I want Glenview kids to be successful,' but do they really get what's going on in Glenview? Or what the daily challenges are? Or what the city's aspirations are? Or what the community needs? Or stuff like that? How important it would be to make sure that kids from there have, you know, educational outcomes that are equal to their peers that are more privileged? Like, no!"

When Khalil was still at Huerta, he had been optimistic about the transition to high school. I asked if he was nervous: "Schools wise? About making good grades? Naw, just paying attention. I pay attention well, I understand stuff." I asked about other students: "I think I'm gonna get along with a lot of kids. I don't think, I'm not a troublemaker. I used to be a hot head but no more." He explained how now, after having fought back against bullying when he was younger, if people make fun of him for anything he just laughs it off. A couple of his friends, Rahul and Snoop, were going to Westside. He was planning on getting a ride to school with Rahul's dad but had to figure out his own way home because

Rahul dropped his seventh period AVID. AVID (Advancement Via Individual Determination) was a national program of support classes for students from underrepresented groups who were taking advanced courses. It was designed to create a community so students didn't feel so isolated and to provide resources for navigating the challenge. None of the students I followed ended up taking AVID classes.

Khalil indicated that when he signed up for high school classes he made the choice not to take as many advanced classes as he was eligible for in order to keep his grades up. When he described the sign-up process, however, it wasn't clear whether, as often happens (Yonezawa, Wells, and Serena, 2002), he had actually been steered into this choice. He said he didn't feel ready for Biology, but in explaining why, he used the transition counselor's words: "She was like, 'it's a lot of reading in there and you got Advanced Writing and you got Geometry' and then I'm playing sports after school and then that means I'm going to be up late getting off from practice ... And then I have to do my regular homework then read a lot for Biology then go to sleep at like 12:00 and do it all over again so I was afraid to ... until I get used to the high school." He planned to take it his sophomore year instead.

On the one hand, this was a sensible decision rooted in Khalil's assessment of how busy he was likely to be and the challenges ahead. On the other, he was a top student who was really academically ambitious. Being in biology might have helped him sustain relationships across his advanced courses, and would have set him up better for college, as it might have for Rahul, Memo, and Jaqueline. By enrolling in advanced math without

Advanced Science, they all effectively became more isolated from peers who were in advanced-level courses and de-tracked for college science majors, despite their strength in math.

I watched one of Khalil's first days of Advanced Integrated Science (a regular level course) at the high school. The class was full, with 40 kids. I sat on a lab stool at a table with a little gas outlet on it. The day's lesson was on observation versus inference and qualitative versus quantitative. The teacher reviewed some basics, then he put a picture up on the smartboard of someone sitting, sweating, with their legs spread out, and asked the students to share observations. A few students, mostly white, offered observations. Then a white student raised their hand and said: "he's a happy slave!" The teachers responded, "Maybe he's a happy slave pulling a block" and then added "I don't think I've ever seen a happy slave but …" The class moved on and students kept sharing answers as the teacher continued to cycle through pictures.

Whiteness infiltrated even seemingly disconnected conversations like this one. It wasn't evident to me that any of the Huerta students picked up on the "happy slave" comment, but unaddressed microaggressions and microassaults like this can produce hostile contexts for students of color in STEM classrooms (Osanloo, Boske, and Newcomb, 2016). While the teacher indicated his discomfort in passing, he did not directly address it with the class beyond this. Persistent inattention to racial microaggressions and white racial frames by schools mean that not only are students of color harmed and marginalized, but white students are provided minimal opportunity to interrogate their racial assumptions and identities (Kohli, Arteaga, and McGovern, 2019). Often white students exit "excellent" schools like Valley

Vista and Westside "functionally illiterate" in matters of race and racism (DiAngelo, 2012). Khalil would talk later about how white students' and teachers' racism and lack of racial awareness shaped his education.

When he entered high school, Khalil was actively trying to make white friends. He talked about this with me and with his Geometry teacher. At Huerta, he liked having friends from a diversity of backgrounds and at Westside he sought to diversify further, but he also imagined having white friends would help him succeed academically and stay out of trouble. "I like having them because, like, at Huerta, with my friends, I would get upset. Like, if someone gave me an A-, I'd get upset. I'd be like, I did all the work. I did everything. Why am I getting an A-, but my friends, everyone else, they all got like Cs and Ds so they'd be like, 'are you serious Khalil?' Like Rahul, he always got Cs and Ds and so he'd be like, 'are you serious? You're upset about an A-?' But these kids, they're upset about an A- too, so I feel like I fit in better." When I asked him in January about how school was going, he told me, "it's cool … I went to school with like no white kids. Come to this school, I know a lot of white kids now … I don't even mess with the Mexicans and the Blacks, they get me in trouble too much. Snoop just got kicked out of this school." Khalil was feeling like he needed to reject his friends from Glenview (a persistent message from Westside school officials) in order to stay out of trouble and succeed in school, but was also having a hard time with white students' racism. He had almost hit a kid on his basketball team. "He kept stereotyping me. Every time he saw me. He'd be like 'what's up rogue? What's up blood? You want some of this purple juice?' I was like man, come on now, but we're cool now." He had visited that student's house with his team. He described how the house had an in-ground trampoline, a pool, batting cages, and a tennis court. After he confronted the white student, he said the harassment "kind of" stopped.

Khalil's Geometry teacher shared her reflections: "Khalil, I sure like a whole lot. I think he's a very sweet kid … I think he feels the separation between himself and most of the rest of the class, I don't know, very acutely, or however you say that, but I think he notices it a lot."

Me: What did he say to you? When he was sitting at this table the other day? Did he say 'I'm segregated over here?' Did he say something like that?

Mrs Cameron: It's entirely possible. He makes a lot of comments like that … some of them are kind of joking … like there was one day where I had added the points wrong on his test, like, I, I just misadded and he really deserved two more points and he was like 'oh,' and then he was like 'oh never mind' and I was like, 'what were you going to say? It's because you're Black?' and he was like 'he he, yeah,' and I was like 'okay, right, 'cause I never made a mistake adding a white kid's test before. Just you.'

As in the moment described earlier in which Khalil said he felt segregated, Mrs Cameron dismissed his concerns. She even mocked them, even though her tone was loving. She revisited the question of his isolation, but attributed it to him: "Khalil doesn't really interact with the rest of his group that much … it's funny because they're grouped … by their grades, so they're in with students who have approximately the same grade ... so he really is with students who have the same level of understanding as he does, but I think he feels like somehow they all get it so much quicker and he doesn't really talk to them." She went on: "I will say, compared to a lot of students from Glenview, Khalil has done pretty well ... He's pretty much maintained a B the whole way through." Khalil, of course, wanted an A. He didn't want Glenview students to be the metric he was compared against, and he didn't want to be doing "pretty well." His feeling that he didn't understand was tied to him wanting to be among the best students, not just "holding his own," but Ms Cameron had anchored her expectations for him in Glenview.

Ms Cameron also laughed at Khalil having told her that he wanted to have more white friends this year: "He was like, it's cool, it's been cool, there are some cool people. I'm like, okay, good, I'm glad you realized that there are actually cool white people out there. You can be friends with them. It's not a big deal. You can hang out." But it was a big deal and Khalil couldn't easily hang out. A cheating incident in Ms Cameron's class reflected just a few of the myriad ways making friends with the majority of the kids in his advanced classes—the white kids—was fraught for Khalil.

When Ms Cameron assigned students to do chapter reviews using a computer program called Sketchpad she told students the school would loan them computers if they didn't have one. Khalil was able to get a loaner computer, but without the knowledge of how to work the technology, he still ended up having problems completing the assignment. He didn't just need to have access to a computer, he needed to purchase specific software. He talked to me about it at the time and years later.

His accounts of what happened were pretty much the same. "I told my mom to buy that shit," he told me, but his mom didn't have any familiarity with computers. "I didn't ever. We didn't have electronics. That's the problem I had in Geometry. They tell me to work off the computer and I'm like, my mom doesn't have a computer. I, I don't know. I've never had a computer. I just started playing around with computers until I came, met Rahul." As a result, Khalil struggled to complete the assignment, "I couldn't get the problems to print from the computer. I could only get like four of them to print so I called this guy and asked him to send me his ... we all have the same propositions and stuff written down so I didn't think it was that big a deal, but she gave us all a zero for it." He had copied off Cam and he, his partner, and another two students his partner had shared their work with had all gotten zeros.

Khalil felt ashamed and withdrew. He took full responsibility on himself and minimized any discussion of how the penalty hurt him, indicating the white students had different expectations on them so it hurt them more. "I felt bad. I mean, for me it took me from a B to a C but for them getting a B is, like, a really big deal. I mean, it didn't mean that much for me, but I felt especially bad for the girl because I guess it took all of them down from an A to a B and for them that's a really big deal because they never get B's." I asked him if he'd ever talked to any of them about it

Khalil: No. No, I don't talk to any of them anymore.

Me: Why? Because they don't talk to you or because you feel bad?

Khalil: Because I feel bad. I see any of them coming and I just put my head down …

Me: Why do you feel so bad?

Khalil: I feel like it's my fault.

Me: But weren't there, like, five people?

Khalil: Yeah, five people … and she gave us all zeros.

Me: But then it wasn't all your fault.

Khalil: I know but I just feel like it is. I've always been like that. Like in basketball if someone doesn't make a shot and I passed them the ball I'm like, I shouldn't have passed them the ball, take me out of the game.

Even though he recognized he had major technology access issues and that these contributed to what happened, Khalil shouldered the responsibility for his white peers' actions and imagined that, ironically, because of their privileges, the consequences were greater for them. He saw them as having more to lose.

In schools such as Westside where honors tracks are dominated by white students, Black students who excel academically become more socially isolated (Fryer and Torelli, 2022). Khalil was struggling with how to participate and persist in this space without putting down and abandoning his friends from Glenview, whom he still loved and felt loyal and connected to, and still relied on in important ways. They were and had been his lifeline after years of moving, and while he wanted to really push himself academically, he didn't want to do it alone. He thought he might make white friends but saw how that option was foreclosed as time went on. As the school seemed to abandon other Glenview students and his friends got successively expelled, he found himself more and more alone. One of the dynamics Valenzuela (1999) has pointed to in her text *Subtractive Schooling* is how school cultures and structures work to fracture and fragment vital social networks between students who are all marginalized, but differently so. Circling back to Jaqueline's point about what it means to be *with us*, the ways that Khalil was heroized and held as an example as he pushed even harder academically seemed to work to further fracture and frustrate his structures of support.

Khalil earned a 4.0 his sophomore year. He was singled out for praise. "People started seeing it … Boys and Girls club reached out and gave me a job and they put my poster up in there. They gave me SAT classes at [the nearby university], they tried to get me in advanced classes and shit … They knew that I was not retarded I guess." But, he said, "shit sucked!" After that year, he started to pull back on school. "After sophomore year I took Advanced Standing Algebra II and the next year I took Pre-Calc. I didn't. I didn't drop. I didn't go down in classes. I just didn't … I didn't spend all the time doing my homework and all that shit. No more. My whole sophomore year. I don't know. It just didn't seem like I was happy." Pressure and social isolation combined with a lot of fear and unknowns about college. "I was still scared to apply for schools … It just seemed like it wasn't going to work and I don't like not having money so I wasn't down to be a broke ass college student. Like, I'm scared to be broke. I've been broke a lot. So, I was like, no."

He was still trying to figure it all out when he ran into a military recruiter on campus: "He just talked to me and I joined …

I never wanted to be a Marine ... It was September of my senior year." After he joined, he dropped most of his classes, including AP Statistics. "I took like three classes senior year: Weight training, English, and one more class. I was only in school for an hour or two every day my senior year and I worked at 7-11 the whole time." Military recruiting actively targets poor students and students of color on high school campuses, with promises of a less financially painful path to college (Quinn and Meiners, 2009). As college prices continue to rise rapidly relative to financial aid, finances are a deep impediment that makes calculations about the payoffs and the costs from college really hard, particularly for students of color who, because of labor market and wage discrimination, tend to see much less return on investment from college degrees than white students do (Libassi, 2018).

Khalil's afterward

When I met up with Khalil after he got out of the Marines, he was staying with Rahul in his dad's house. They were both taking classes at community college. For biology, they were diagraming the rough and smooth endoplasmic reticulum. Their work was on a whiteboard on the wall of Rahul's garage. Khalil's mom had been forced to move out of Glenview by rising rents and was now an hour away. He was thinking about becoming a US Marshall. Despite his love for Huerta, Khalil felt like the school let him down, that they had "played" him. "I think Huerta would have set me up for success if I went to [the local charter high school that targets Glenview students], but not ... Westside." He felt like one of the problems was "I was, like, the smartest kid until I got to Westside, so I think, that's not my fault, I'm waiting, like all the classes I'm waiting for other people to catch up, so that's not my fault, so I feel like I got played." But this wasn't just about whether he was prepared—Khalil was clearly able to compete at advanced levels at Westside—it was also about social isolation, "I don't know, all the other kids, 'cause I never had any friends in any of my classes. Any of my classes. Rahul was in my Geometry class. That's the only, like, friend I had in my classes growing up, in like, all, everybody was white. I'd have to take, like, I'd have to take dumber classes to be with my friends ... I hated high school." Khalil's indication that Huerta would have set him up to go to a charter that was rigorous, but almost one hundred percent students of color, points to the myriad ways racism, tracking, and whiteness in the classroom (and broader school structures) shaped his isolation and eventual disengagement.

As we talked, other details of what had happened between sophomore year and junior year started to emerge. Khalil's mom lost her housing and had to move, and he was harassed and terrified by the Westside police. "I ever mention," he asked me, "I got pulled over in Westside and they thought Shayla stole the car? We were, like, 15 and 16, Shayla had a driver's permit ... he pulled us over and no one got out of the car. He didn't get out of the car and then more cop cars came and we're like, 'fuck,' so then you know they made a big scene ... they're like, put your hands up!" The police had left as soon as they realized the car wasn't stolen. The police didn't wait for their mom or ticket Shayla for driving on a permit, actions both children understood as meaning the police recognized their actions were racist. He also told me about another time, close to that, "in Westside, I'm walking home one time and they ... one drew his weapon, and he was just, just scanning the ground to see if I dropped anything?" This kind of police harassment, terrorizing, and abuse—the ways he was subject to state violence—made it even more difficult to deal with the white kids.

Khalil was 22 years old and had just returned from the Marines, having survived all he had, being an incredibly strong student all his life, having been super clean cut until after he enlisted—no drugs, no alcohol, no smoking, no stealing, nothing—and yet he was treated, persistently, with suspicion and fear. "I can see it on people's faces too, they're scared of me. I don't like that." And he told me stories. One was of the time "I was trying on this belt in Macy's and this motherfucker thought I was stealing. I was like, dude, I wouldn't even steal a fucking candy bar and you're over here harassing me because I'm trying on a belt." Another time, he and Rahul went to buy a gun at the gun store and the owner "acted like we wanted to steal, like, I just, you could feel it, like, stop looking. Why does everybody have to look at me 'cause I walk into the gun store? We can buy guns too! I just stay quiet," he said, "but it makes me mad, 'cause white people don't see it."

In one of his community college classes, Khalil's teacher had gotten up in his face and started pointing her finger at him after he expressed a difference of opinion about protein shakes. Other students reported her behavior, but he was still angry about it. In a way I never quite understood, it connected to something that happened sophomore year. "She puts her fingers in my face … I've never raised my voice at her … that's why I stopped caring about grades though, because I feel like it's impressing the teacher. I don't want to impress the teacher. I just want to learn." He gave philosophy, which he was studying at the community college, as an example of something he liked learning, "Plato and shit, in the cave, like what's really real and stuff, so I think that's cool, but I don't care if he gives me an A … I don't care about people's grades anymore … teachers fucked that up for me." I asked when. "When I got a 4.0 and I don't know, I don't know." As Khalil had reached the goal he had been aiming for social isolation, encounters with racist policing, and economic insecurity had unsettled his confidence in that path.

In college, he was also taking a politics class. "When my teacher brings up police. Like, I hate talking about police. Police and Black people. Because white kids do not understand it … they just don't think cops harass Black people. Like, it's just, 'he shouldn't have been moving.'" He described having gone to a party with one of the white girls from one of his classes and how "there was a bunch of, like, white jocks were there. I don't get that. I don't get why people can't just be chill…. I mean, I know I'm Black. Naw, you guys don't have any Black friends. That's cool. I'm the only one. I'm American too but like the whole, you can feel it. The party stops … I tell her, your friends are kinda like, and she's like, 'no, they're really chill!' and I'm like 'okay, never mind' and she's like 'no, he's just like that because …' and I'm like 'allright, cool, that's cool,' and then when she invited me again I'm like 'Hell no! I don't want to chill with your friends anymore!'… Like I can see them talking shit … I'll think in my head, like, should I get mad? That's what I think, I'm like, nope. I'm gonna be allright … I called Rahul that night too. I was like, 'should I get mad?' and he was like 'No, just chill out, it's cool,' so I went back to [his house] but, like, shit pisses me off …. If I would have walked in and I was white they wouldn't have turned, they would have been like 'oh, nice to meet you.'"

The friendships Khalil temporarily sought to leave behind as a way of escaping criminalization turned out to be vital to surviving, processing, and resisting the racist (de)segregation, displacement, and dispossession he endured. Rahul was like an anchor for Khalil (and vice versa) amidst persistent "root shock" (Fullilove, 2004) and his ongoing displacement. He taught him to use the computer, loaned him a computer, gave him somewhere to go when he got out of the Marines, and so on. And Khalil's mom was an advocate and quasi-parental figure for Rahul. They couldn't be more different, but there they were, in Rahul's basement, surrounded by Rahul's bong collection, studying the rough and smooth endoplasmic reticulum, Khalil stressing about how hard he could push Rahul at the gym without breaking him. Khalil worked at the gym, planning to one day open his own business. He also made music—music that critiqued police brutality, called out Donald Trump's racism, and slammed liberal colorblind politics "'racism doesn't exist?' Yeah, that's a lie and a white joke."

6
Talli: You stay with your own kind

As part of an 8th grade biographies project at Valley Vista Middle School, a newspaper reporter came to talk to the students about interviewing. He was a white man, and he sat on the edge of a table in the front of the packed library in front of row upon row of mostly white students. He told stories about his adventures with dangerous situations, people, and places—almost all were focused on Black people, people of color, and Indigenous people, in geographies beyond and within the US. At the end of his talk, a student asked him if he had any happy stories. He described interviewing an indigenous woman who was the last person to speak her language. This devastating moment of language loss stemming from systemic genocide and dispossession he presented as "happy" because "nobody was shooting and nobody was getting hurt." The students in the room were entranced. At the end, their questions focused almost entirely on the reporter himself—what he had experienced, how he had survived, how his family felt, and what he thought. Talli was one of these students. She sat at the back. She was fashionably dressed, long hair down her back. She raised her hand during Q and A and asked, "What's it like interviewing someone you know has killed somebody?"

At Valley Vista, Talli and her friends hung out against the wall, apart from the "popular kids" and the "drama kids." Talli had fallen out with one of her best friends, Lucy--"This Persian girl, she's, like, very hyper, she's a very eccentric person."--after a failed attempt to become friends with the "popular kids." At the beginning of eighth grade they had decided together to try to join the group. Shortly thereafter, Talli had yelled at a girl who she said was talking shit behind her back, and that girl "told her sister who was in the popular group." Talli then "had no chance of getting in," but Lucy, her friend, still did. As Talli described it, Lucy was "more willing to sacrifice the friends she already had than I was." "Lucy started hanging out with them ... so I was just like, 'screw you, I'll go hang out with people who like me!'"

The small group of friends Talli did hang out with was more diverse than most of the other groups at Valley Vista and included, at varying times, students who were Korean, Tongan, and Black. At lunch at Valley Vista, they would sit on the blacktop in a small cluster of three or four, a couple of them with backs up against a classroom wall. One of her Tongan friends, Nina, had parents who were both active in Pacific Islander and Christian organizing in Glenview. They ran a church-based youth program that included open mic performances, slam poetry, and food out of a small church at the end of River Street. They also helped lead programs at Huerta but, like many parents with the resources (time, literacy, knowledge, relationships), they had transferred their children out of the district.

For Talli, the hardest thing about starting high school, by far, had been the social transition. She had lost her best friends, as near as she could figure, because of how the school was segregated. "I'm still talking to my friends, like Nina and Ellie but, um, we're not close anymore because … when you come here everybody kind of goes into their own ethnic groups, like, the school is diverse and, like, integrated, but … you know the white people eat on the grass and the minorities eat over by the library lunch area, where the food's being sold. It's sad because I did lose, like, a couple of really good friends." She explained how, when they first got to Westside, she had asked her friends, "Why aren't you eating lunch with us on the grass?" and they said. "we don't really feel like we belong there" and "it just kind of happened." I asked if she would ever eat over there with them and she said she wouldn't feel comfortable: "You get weird looks and stuff." Nina and Ellie had extensive relationships with other students from Glenview through church, youth nights, and other activities their families were a part of, and their relationships with Westside youth, despite having gone to school there for many years, were much more limited.

Talli had tried to hang out with the broader group of students from Glenview that included her old friends but "it was frustrating because Black people were just like, 'why you trying to act ghetto' … and I was like 'I'm not trying to act that way, that's just how I say it.'" I asked her what kind of stuff she'd been saying and she told me, "I don't know, like you say stuff in the ghetto, like telling 'gimme some' or 'let me get' … like, not talking proper English and, like, people were like, 'why you saying shit like that?

You're not ghetto. You're white or whatever.'" Talli seemed confused and sad that her friendships had broken apart, but it was also clear she lacked basic racial competence and was carrying fears and stereotypes that put up real roadblocks to hanging out with Glenview students. Talli both misused and appropriated African American and other local Glenview languages. This was an area of critical importance for many Glenview youth, whose linguistic, cultural, and community resources were often under threat at the high school. White students' mocking, mimicking, and clumsy attempts to use these languages were (and were felt, lived, and understood as) insults, appropriations, and dispossessions—taking and abuse of things that did not belong to them (Hill, 1999).

Talli explained that she had grown up in a household that was "pretty liberal … pretty open about, you know, gay people" but that "Blacks, at the time [my mom] grew up it was like, you know, Negros, you know, like that's all bad, like, minorities and stuff like that." She said her mom had told her to make up her own mind and "I just kind of came to the conclusion that I don't have a problem with colored people." While Talli rejected her mothers' overt racism, she used offensive and antiquated language ("colored people") to do so. Talli had decided she didn't want to be racist, and she felt some kinship with a couple of students of color, but she didn't have the tools to speak and act in ways that were not harmful, let alone understand how she and other students persisted in, contributed to, or might contest structural racism and white supremacy. This didn't just hurt her friends of color and the broader communities of students they were a part of, it hurt her as well, but her whiteness and wealth isolated her from many of the consequences of this harm. Talli was facing difficult situations at home. Youth from Glenview offered her support, but Talli didn't have the tools to meaningfully reciprocate, or even to avoid causing harm. Feeling racially ostracized and unable to recognize and thus repair her own violence, she cut herself off from this source of support.

Talli's mom was a recovering alcoholic. Talli had spent a lot of her childhood taking care of her and cleaning up after her. She described one time when her mom drove "very intoxicated" with Talli in the car. "We were up, like, driving back from Tahoe and, like, she got pulled over in a parking lot and, like, there was a Motel across the street and the officer was like, he gave me the keys and I remember this really vividly, I was like seven or eight. He was like, 'don't let your mother have the keys until the morning' … we stayed in the motel next door and, like, she slept it off, and then we left in the morning." This story was a vivid example of the kind of life-changing immunity white and wealthy families could get from legal consequences. Talli's mom should (by law) have been jailed. Talli might have been removed from her custody (Dettlaff and Boyd, 2021). They could have been under constant CPS supervision. Talli wasn't free from consequences—she was in danger, had to play an adult role as a child, and was left in the hands of someone in no shape to care for her. But the structural consequences for her family would have been much more severe had her mother faced criminal charges (Ferguson, 1995).

Talli explained how taking care of her mom had shaped her into a person who tried to take care of everyone else—keeping her friends from driving drunk, holding their hair while they puked, and so on. Talli and her mom lived in a big house in Westside and her dad lived in a trailer in nearby Castleton, "so I go from a nice house in Westside into, you know, that atmosphere. I'm able, I'm lucky enough to be able to see it and balance it out from both ends you know." She explained that her parents had helped found a tech company before they split up and they had "a couple houses in the area." Her dad now worked in a coffee shop, having unsuccessfully started his own company. She had gone through lots of therapy to help her process the divorce: "They would tell me, 'it's not your fault that your parents are getting divorced, you know, it's not your fault that your mom drinks' and you only believe that to a certain extent but, like, I know now that it's not my fault." Talli described the house she lived in with her mom as big, empty, and lonely.

While the wealth gaps between Westside and Glenview students were extreme, racialized wealth gaps are important in understanding how inequality operates in the United States. Wealth describes assets that are owned, often inherited, as opposed to income or wages (Oliver and Shapiro, 2006). Talli's family's multiple houses would have been worth many millions of dollars. Her parents' incomes might be low while they may still hold a lot of wealth. Much wealth results from dispossession—land grants of stolen native land, wealth built through the use of stolen African and Indigenous labor, coffers built on stolen Indigenous gold, minerals, and oil (Grosfoguel, 2005) historically. Without reparations—the process of returning stolen wealth—the wealth is free to be passed on, inherited, and used for projects and processes that are then represented as earned through hard work and intelligence. Practices such as segregation, redlining, inequitable pay, and housing lending discrimination have further concentrated wealth in white families through systemically unequal treatment. Regardless of its source, the wealth in Westside did not exist independently of or separately from the dispossession in Glenview. The practices of resource hoarding and segregation described throughout this text, systemically financially enriched Westside residents, neighborhoods, city, and schools (whether through property values, educational prestige, tax revolt, exclusive planning decisions, or cheap labor), at the expense of Glenwood residents, schools, and city.

The recession and the sub-prime crisis that was happening as these students entered high school wiped out the Black and Brown wealth built up since the 1970s, when the last recession did the same (Oliver and Shapiro, 2008). In the 1950s, white flight stripped middle-class Black and Brown wealth as white homeowners built wealth on subsidized loans and racial exclusion. Free trade agreements that produced markets for US goods and wealth for US companies drove people off their land in Mexico and Central America and compelled migration in the 1990s. These are a few among many examples of interrelationship. I do not know for how long Talli, Cam, or Amy's families had their wealth, how much of it was inherited and passed down. Talli didn't know, "people are like, 'what do your parents do?' 'Uh, nothing.' 'How do you live in West Westside?' 'No idea.' You know, [my mom,] she's independently wealthy. I've never seen my mom work, like, a day in her life. I'm always like, you should get a job at a boutique or something, 'naw, I'm okay.'"

Me: What does she do all day then?

Talli: Her nails. Sits around. She's like, 'I'm so busy.' I'm like, 'doing what? You have three maids and, like, a dog that you walk every two weeks. I don't know what you do all day. Shop?'

Part of wealth's power rests in the capacity to disguise its origins.

I asked Talli if there was anything she had learned from coming to this school. "I thought I'd like it a lot more than I did coming here," she told me, "I guess I didn't really realize how segregated it is, 'cause I always got the impression because they say, like, oh yeah, we, we're a district school, we bus kids in from Glenview, that sort of stuff, it is integrated, but it's segregated, you know, and it's like, I didn't realize there was such an unspoken rule that, you know … unspoken law, I guess, that you stay with your own kind …. It kind of helps me to see how other people view the world and, like, if you're out in the world, how racist people can be racist and how, like, you, you see the world through skin colors and that stuff." Talli was used to being in a context (Valley Vista) where whiteness was so dominant Talli was not challenged on her racism, nor were her colorblind frameworks disrupted. At Westside, whiteness was still dominant, but she was also called out on her racism and in a context where students of color could more effectively distance from harmful behavior from white peers. This pushed her, at first, to feel like she was becoming more racist.

Talli hadn't just noticed the segregation in her friend group, she'd noticed it in her classes as well. "I'm in AS English … I noticed the other day when I was with my friend talking about it, there's not one colored person in my class." She said her World Studies class was also "pretty much only white people," but her Algebra class was "pretty ghetto." I asked what she meant. "I wish I had a better word for it, um, like there's a lot of Spanish people, um, Hispanic people, and, um, Black people, and I'm one of maybe three white kids in my class and they're all girls. I wish I had a better word to generalize it but ghetto's kind of the term that's used." "Ghetto" was a term that was used commonly among the white students. It was not commonly used by students of color, not in this way. When used by white students it was largely used pejoratively. When used by students of color, it could be a way of naming structural violence or claiming space (Paperson, 2010). Talli knew she didn't have the language, but if she wanted tools to deepen her racial literacy, she would have had to seek them out, and it's not quite clear where she would have gone without putting the burden of educating her on her peers of color.

Despite Talli's struggle with racially respectful language and frameworks, she said she felt "more comfortable with the ghetto kids than I do with the white kids, just 'cause they're a little bit more real, they understand life more, they're a little more, like, I don't know, just street smart or whatever." When they had done the Dialogue Day, she had stayed back during the cross-the-line activity when the facilitators had said "cross the line if you had a childhood." She recounted how a lot of the people who had held back with her were Fijian and Tongan and they had offered support, "they were like, 'I got your back, I'm here if you need anything' which was cool."

To "have a childhood" functions as a form of privilege and protection afforded to some youth and not others. Young people of color are often criminalized, punished as adults, and seen as threats from very young ages. This is often done in opposition to imagined white innocence and the imagined need for the protection of white youth (Meiners, 2016). Talli was deprived of childhood by her mother's drinking, which forced her to take on many adult responsibilities. She was also, however, still afforded childhood by the systems that hyper-surveilled and punished many of her peers of color, particularly Black and Brown children, many of whom were struggling with similar issues at home.

Talli was aware of what had happened to her and how hard it had been, but she wasn't aware of her privileges, racism, or ignorance. At the same time, Talli was aware of at least some of the stereotypes that, not just people from her school, but also she herself carried: "In all honesty, and I'm sure a lot of the white people from high school thought this, like, understand nothing I'm saying is racist or anything like that because I don't feel that way, but I'm just saying like a lot of the white kids were probably like [she inhaled through her teeth] 'it's a ghetto school,' 'it's a public school,' you know, 'they bus kids in,' 'I'm gonna watch my stuff because it's going to get stolen by one of them' type things. I would never, you know, say like, I would never disrespect a person because of their color of their skin or say anything like that, but like, it's kinda always there in the back of your mind as hard as you try it not be, like, what skin color are you and how much money you have, it always plays in eventually."

Talli did talk about some of this with her friends, and she drew on those conversations as she talked to me. She had different conversations with her white friends than with her friends of color, "like maybe, you know, with my white friends it'd be like, 'oh yeah, you know, I'm gonna make sure my stuff doesn't get stolen' or 'oh yeah, it's a public school so you know it's, it's gonna be ghetto or whatever' and like, with my, like, friends, that, like, ah, colored or whatever, they'd be like, 'oh yeah, all my family goes there,' or, 'I went there I'm excited to play sports.' I think maybe they had a more of a positive outlook on it ... like, they never saw it as a ghetto school, like the white people saw it as a ghetto school." White students often started with the presumption that neither their stuff nor their bodies were safe around Glenview youth in ways that were racist, hurtful, and damaging. Talli's comments sum up many of the tensions in "desegregation" at Westside High. While white racism and privilege often made Westside a dispossessive and harmful space for Glenview students, there were also lots of resources, family histories with the school, and individual teachers that Glenview students valued. The school offered opportunities in competitive sports, advanced classes, electives, materials, staffing, and facilities (however limited access was) that were unimaginable in Glenview schools and held real value.

Talli had been to Glenview once, to drop someone off. "One time I went there with Monica, who's Tongan, we were picking up Lisa, whose also Tongan I think, and we drove over from Westside. We were there for like two hours. I remember there being bars on the windows and I'd never seen bars on windows except in other countries and I remember, this sounds horrible, but I remember not seeing really any white people and I remember, I don't know if I'm just making this up, but I remember feeling like I wanted to get out of there. And I remember my friend, this guy, I don't remember his name, but I remember him saying that he couldn't sleep the night before because of the gunshots and thinking that sounded like something from a movie. I mean. It was probably true, but it sounded like a movie. I don't know. I always feel like it was like a statistic. Like Glenview was a statistic. The place was a statistic."

Talli had read the fact that students were "bused in" from Glenview as a sign that her school might be meaningfully integrated, and she seemed to think it was something the school did in a benevolent way, "they bus kids in." She could see segregation operating all around her, but again, the link she didn't have, at least not explicitly, was understanding herself and her school as racist. She didn't understand that students were bused in because their elders in Glenview had protested, demonstrated, sued, and pursued all manner of political action to address the deep educational inequality caused by white flight, racist local educational policy, and persistent opportunity hoarding and white resistance. She didn't realize many Westside parents and district officials had resisted (and continued to resist) desegregating these schools or that they had resisted (and continued to resist) more equitable public funding of K-12 schools throughout the state through anti-tax legislation and the use of private foundations to fund education for their own children. She didn't know the history of racism in (or beyond) her community or the decades of work required to create spaces of beauty, joy, community, and care in Glenview amid hostility and loss. How could she respect and be present with her friends, if all she was able to see when she looked at their city was bars on the windows and her own fear?

Talli wasn't just socially frustrated at the high school, she was also academically frustrated. She had dropped out of French because "Ms Klaus is annoying", and she was struggling with her math teacher because felt humiliated and degraded in her class. She described a moment when she asked a question and her teacher responded, "you don't know? You don't' know what this times this is?" Talli said, "I was like, 'no! I don't! I'm sorry! I'm retarded! Want to, like, tell me so I can sit back down and feel like crap?' And she was like 'excuse me?' and I just had to walk away." Grappling with a learning disability and frustrated in class, Talli threw back at her teacher the offensive and ableist language she imagined her teacher's treatment of her implied. She liked her other classes, but felt like, on multiple levels, Westside wasn't working for her. Yet, Talli's outbursts weren't punished like Rahul's were (see next chapter). She wasn't suspended, or even sent to the office. And she had options. As she began to think about leaving, one of the schools she considered was Charter Prep, a nearby charter high school that boasted about its diversity, lack of tracking, and progressive curriculum.

It seemed white students who were tracked low at Westside often sought other options. Lower tracks were marked as "ghetto" or primarily for students of color, indicating to white students these spaces were not for them—just as happened with disciplinary spaces at the school. Amy was paying for summer school classes to get out of Algebra and Talli, like a number of other white students in the lower tracks I spoke to or knew of, was considering Charter Prep, private school, or alternative school options. White students were aware of being among the few white students in their classes, and often expressed embarrassment about their placement and awareness of their racial isolation. If students couldn't take summer school or transfer out, they would sometimes petition to move into a higher-level course, although with course placement now tied explicitly to standardized test scores, this was often unsuccessful. Talli had multiple reasons for wanting to transfer; her social isolation and placement in lower track classes were among those reasons.

Charter and private high schools offered one alternative for students looking to leave Westside. Three prominent charter high schools were Elite, a boarding school primarily serving top-performing Glenview students; Ivy Prep, a charter targeting Glenview students with a social justice and equity focus run by the nearby university; and Skyward, a charter that boasted of its diversity, lack of tracking, and creative pedagogy. Nationally, charter school quality varies widely (Zimmer, Buddin, Smith, and Duffy, 2019). While there were many pedagogically and politically innovative things happening at these local charters, their test scores (which are not a good measure of learning, but are what schools are measured by) varied. Like other programs (such as SWAP) that create limited opportunities for small groups of students, these schools did give some families educational options, but they also siphoned resources out of traditional public schools serving high numbers of Glenview students, and students of color more broadly (Fabricant and Fine, 2012). Undermining efforts to make tracks more racially balanced, local charters also gave white students like Talli, who were unhappy with their track placement, somewhere else to go.

For a student like Talli, had she gotten into the tenth-grade transfer lottery, Charter Prep may have offered a meaningful alternative. Talli was queer but not out yet. Westside High had no meaningful programming or administrative action around sexuality or gender identity. Some lesbian, gay, bi, or queer students were open as couples, but there was no explicitly anti-heterosexist statement-making, programming, or curriculum, and the entire curricular apparatus was largely heteronormative; although, as with race, this was often implicit rather than explicit. LGBTQIA+ students often found LGBTQIA+ teachers who would support them, but this happened on the side. In contrast, Charter Prep had an explicit policy and statement about gender and sexual inclusivity, a gender and name change form posted to their website, and a clear harassment and bullying policy. They also had explicit statements acknowledging the racist, sexist, heterosexist, and ableist discrimination their students face in the society we exist in. Thus, their approach to systemic gender and sexuality related oppression, racism, and structural violence (Quinn and Meiners, 2009) was much more proactive. At Westside High, inequalities were acknowledged but not named as systemic violence or oppression, and white, heteronormative, cis, normatively-able, male bodies continued as the de-facto center of the school.

Talli's afterward

I talked to Talli ten years later, over Zoom. She was living in LA with her girlfriend. She had left Westside and gone to two private schools before eventually enrolling in a community college dual enrollment program and then "from there I just ended up getting my GED." She officially "graduated" from one of the Westside Unified School District high schools, but did so through the test. After high school, she backpacked Europe, went to Morocco, "and then worked with horses for a while." From there she was headed to Florida and then "after that I'm going to Europe, on a one-way ticket this time." The reality of Talli's wealth meant that, for her, not completing high school or not going to college did not mean a struggle to survive or support others on low-wage work; rather, it afforded a set of adventures, learning, and travel experiences that, in their own way, set her up for a labor market that valued these things.

I asked Talli about what she remembered of high school. "I remember being miserable there. I remember hating it. The way I remember, I had this diverse group of friends at Valley Vista … and I remember when I went to Westside it was so segregated and so divided … I remember losing a lot of friends to that. I just lost a lot of friends and it was really sad and I was really sad about it." She talked about Dialogue Day, how seven students didn't cross the line; "afterwards we all got together and talked and it was like race or color or any of that it didn't matter … it lasted like a week or two but not really even that because the school was still how it was and we all just fit back into that." Talli thought Dialogue Day should have happened every year, that it shouldn't just be for freshmen. For Talli, that day was a model of the work schools like Westside should be doing.

We spoke just after Trump's election. She thought Westside was wasting its potential to make some kind of meaningful difference: "With everything that's going on right now, with the killing of Black people by the police and with the elections … schools like Westside that are in a position to, that have all these kids coming together, maybe for the first time, that the way they're doing it now, it isn't working and they need to do it better. They have the chance. They have the chance to teach kids how to be in a community together. They have the chance to teach them what's right and what's wrong. Because I think it's too late to change the adults. I mean, we can't change the police who are shooting Black men and we can't change Trump and all the things he says about Mexicans, but we can teach the students that its wrong. We can teach them how to be different." I asked her why she thought this didn't happen: "Because they're so focused on numbers and on producing results and because the teachers aren't paid well enough and they just don't take the time to think about the fact that they have people here, that these are people, and so they focus on the test scores and on getting the right numbers, they make everyone into numbers, instead of focusing on teaching them. Instead of helping them learn about each other and learn to live together or understand each other. They just focus on the tests, and I guess also because it's so easy for them to get sued or to lose their funding or to get in trouble."

She talked about Valley Vista in a way she hadn't before, as a space that was more open. "I feel like Valley Vista was a place that made it possible for people to be their funky, freaky selves, that kind of embraced that. I mean, there were always the cool kids and whatever but there were murals and dragons on the walls and the teachers made space for us to be weird, I mean there were the kids who liked Led Zeppelin and wore tie dyes and it was just, everyone could kind of be who they were but it's not like that now …. It's all grey and tan and there are no murals or colors and the classrooms all have smartboards and every kid's hooked up to a laptop and the desks are all in rows. I mean, we used to sit facing each other." And she remembered her eighth-grade teacher, "who pulled me aside when I was starting to hang out with the cool kids and was like 'what are you doing Talli? Is this really who you want to be?' He's also the first teacher who told me I was smart, who said that, even though I was dyslexic,

I was smart, and that meant so much, that changed my life. He's one of those teachers who if you could just clone him and make thousands and thousands of him …. So he became the vice principal, and I went back, I don't remember why, I was visiting someone, and he was there in his office and had his door open and he remembered my name and everything. But high school, I don't know, I remember being miserable there. I remember hating it."

Learning objective 4: Dispossession

Dispossession is really just a fancy word for taking or stealing. I use it instead of these other terms because it helps point to some theories that are helpful in understanding how this taking or stealing happens. One is the idea of "accumulation by dispossession" (Harvey, 2005). This points to the understanding that one of the ways the economic system (capitalism) resolves crises is by dispossession—by taking things that were previously publicly held and privatizing them, for example public land, water, prisons, schools, housing, utilities, and so on. Dispossession is particularly useful for making profit when there is a crisis of accumulation. This occurs when the owners of capital hold excess capital (money) but not enough market (not enough people with means or desire to use or buy). Privatization gives capital somewhere to go, some way to make money and grow. Basically, a few people have so much of the overall pool of money that there is no way for them to make more money because there are not enough people left with enough money to buy from them. The solution is to take a public asset, for example, a school, make it into a private or semi-private resource, for example a privately run charter school. You then "invest" in this asset and get a return by collecting taxpayer dollars and providing educational services for less cost than the tax money you collect. This process strips resources away from the public (all of us) and puts them in private hands. Gentrification, a process of flipping neighborhoods from one race-class group to another, can be a systemic form of accumulation by dispossession. Gentrification often entails the state-facilitated privatization of public housing and schools; seizure and redevelopment of private and public assets utilized by the poor; and facilitation of such displacement by undermining protections such as rent control. Dispossession can also refer to loss of rights, freedoms, mobility, and status via criminalization, illegalization, and racialization. Importantly, dispossession is an ongoing process—it is not just static fixed resources that are being seized. The things being seized, such as places and schools, are the products of people's collective, creative labor (Fine and Ruglis, 2009; Fabricant and Fine, 2012).

As you read the next three chapters, think about the following three questions:

1) If dispossession is a taking, who is taking what from whom? What are some different kinds of dispossession you see evident in these stories? (For example economic, language, education, body, knowledge, movement?) Who are the actors involved in these processes and what are they doing? Are there deeper root causes contributing to their actions?

2) When I discuss dispossession I say that part of what is being taken is "collective creative labor." What I mean by this is that things like neighborhoods, languages, and cultures are not just fixed and static things, but things people have worked to create together. What examples do you see in these stories of collective, creative labor? Explain. Why might it matter to name the labor involved in creating these instead of just treating them as fixed or static things?

3) What of the dispossession you see evidenced in these stories do you think could be meaningfully addressed by schools? How? What do you think might be beyond the scope of schools? Why? Are there any ways schools might still have a role in these broader changes? Explain.

7
Rahul: Fuck this school

I walked out of Mr Howard's inauguration day class and I ran into Rahul. He came up to me looking for a dollar for something: "I'm thinking about taking off," he said, "I think I'm going home."

Me: Why?

Rahul: 'Cause school's stupid.

He turned heel and quickly walked away. I followed him, walking by his side. He wouldn't look at me for a long time. Then we stood outside his Geometry class, leaning against the rail.

"I don't want to go to this class because it makes me angry. I never understand what's going on in there and it makes me mad."

We stood there for a while, watching the people on the quad, then somehow we ended up going to Geometry, both of us. It was obvious that he hated being here. He had no idea what was going on. His head was down. He had nothing to do with his group. He was just there, combing his long hair with his fingers, wearing his oversized black and gold Scarface shirt that said RESPECT in big letters. I could feel the futility of his presence as they talked about pi. It wasn't anything that was beyond his capacity. He could do the math. But he had been suspended so much already, missed so much school, cut so much, and been so thoroughly alienated and excluded in this class, he was completely checked out. At the end of the period, he stormed out as fast as he could.

They never work with me: Group work and micro-segregations

I had been watching Rahul in his Geometry class all year. Early on, Rahul sat with his best friend from Huerta, Khalil, and Gio, a Latinx student also from Huerta who spent his whole eighth-grade year sliding around on those roller shoes with wheels on the back. Everyone else in the class was white except one Black student and a South Asian student. A week into the semester, however, Mrs Cameron made a seating chart that left Rahul at a table by himself with the three white students from Westside. They were learning sequencing. As they started working, he looked good, comfortable, and alert. He had done his homework and it seemed like he understood what was going on. Mrs Cameron reviewed sequencing on the smart board and called on students to answer parts of the problem. She called on Rahul and he confidently answered. He got the material. Groupwork followed the lesson. I could see Rahul leaning, trying to work with the boys across the table. They both had curly blonde hair and J-Crew wardrobes. They acknowledged him, even talked to him a few times, but it was clear they were working with each other, not with him. They seemed to discount him. It was subtle, but they would turn towards one another, almost talking into each other's ears, and Rahul would be leaning across the table, trying to see what they were working on, trying to hear what they were saying.

Eventually, Rahul seemed to give up, not just on working with them, but on the class in general. He put his head down on his crossed arms on his desk. Every once and a while he would pop up suddenly to see what was going on. Still, his classmates didn't acknowledge him. At Huerta, Rahul excelled in math, testing into Geometry, an advanced course, even though he had begun to get in trouble at school. One day I asked Maria and Jaqueline if they felt like anyone had changed since middle school. Jaqueline talked about Rahul: "I've known him since fifth grade and, first of all, he's lost a lot of weight since then, not to be messed up, but he did and that's part of it, but he was smart then and then in sixth grade he started getting in a lot of fights … It was like, in fifth grade he was there and then in sixth grade he was in trouble and he started smoking then in seventh grade he was like smoking all the time and then in eighth grade he was just almost gone and then now he's really gone. I mean, he's just like not even here anymore."

The white students' exclusion of Rahul from their Geometry groupwork persisted. A week later, when Mrs Cameron came around asked, "are you all done?"

Rahul: No.

Mrs Cameron: You all have to be done before I'll sign off. You're supposed to be working in a group.

Rahul: They never work with me.

Mrs Cameron: Well, did you ask them for help?

Rahul: No, but they never work with me.

Mrs Cameron: Well, this time I want you all to work together, help each other.

Mrs Cameron positioned Rahul as a receiver of help rather than someone who might contribute something useful to his group. The students turned to him. One of the girls reached across the boy who still wasn't talking to Rahul, and in a small voice started giving him the answers he didn't have.

While Rahul's isolation in this class was the most extreme, Khalil was also concerned with how he was treated. One of the white boys, Brandon, who had been at Rahul's table, was moved to Khalil's in the next iteration of the seating chart. He tried, unsuccessfully, to trade seats with another student, indicating that he didn't want that table. They were in the midst of correcting homework when Mrs Cameron stopped by Khalil's table to ask Khalil why he wasn't working with the group. "I'm kind of, like, segregated," he replied. I didn't hear her full response, but she talked about him self-segregating and encouraged him to work with his group.

While white students grouping together in ways that systematically exclude, erase, and ignore students of color is common, the onus is usually placed on students of color to address this exclusion (Tatum, 2017). As frequently happens, Mrs Cameron identified segregation and exclusion as Khalil and Rahul's doing, not problems of whiteness and racism manifesting in her classroom, despite both students having used clear language to identify a problem to her. Students of color were blamed for isolating themselves when they sought support from one another in the face of exclusion and invisibilization by white students.

Fuck Geometry! I've never got an F in math!

Exactly a month after I first saw Rahul get shut out of his group, I was walking by when I saw him bolt out of Geometry. He was walking fast, holding to the wall, his back to the class. He was just leaving, head down so that his hair almost covered his face. His face was frozen, falling. He dodged to the back, behind the buildings, away from the people. I followed and called to him. I called to him again. He was walking fast, kicking up dirt with his feet. Finally, I caught up with him and I looked at his face. It was tight with trying to hold back rage, anger, frustration, sadness.

Rahul: Fuck Geometry! I got Fs on all my quizzes.

Me: How many?

Rahul: Like five.

His tone was stressed, a little bit defiant, a little bit sad.

Rahul: My dad's gonna kill me. I never got an F in math! I got an F in World Studies. I got an F in Geometry. And I got a D in English. I never got a D in English or an F in math in my life!

By the time I got to ask Mrs Cameron about Rahul, he had too many absences to get credit for the course. Mrs Cameron had called home twice: "I talked to dad and then, I don't know who I talked to the other day ... a brother or cousin or an older sounding person." I asked her about how he had otherwise been in terms of social and academic preparedness in her class. "Well," she answered, "let's just start off with I'd be very surprised if Rahul's not smoking a considerable amount of marijuana … Based on the amount of marijuana t-shirts that he owns … I think Rahul has more of an investment than just enjoying the t-shirt … and he's just so tuned out so much of the time and has been since day one."

Rahul was aware of people's perceptions of him. At 5'11" he was taller than almost all his peers. His respect for and engagement with both hip hop and reggae cultures, core pieces of how he understood and connected with his identity, were read as criminal and deviant by his teacher and used to justify his persistent failure. Years later, I asked Rahul about his exclusion in this class and he took it on himself. "I know I'm not the most approachable person," he told me. "Obviously, from my looks, I look like a mean ass dude, that's what I get a lot of the time, so I understood why, though, honestly, I didn't care when I was that age. I didn't care about other people's opinions at all." Whether he cared or not, these kinds of judgements shaped how school officials perceived and treated Rahul. Asian-American and Pacific Islander students have organized in myriad ways against the systemic discrimination they face in and beyond schools (Kwon, 2008). What Rahul was facing wasn't just about him, but systemic mistreatment and misrecognition, but he internalized and assumed responsibility for the discrimination. It wasn't that his teacher was wrong, he did smoke weed, but so, as described by Cam, did lots of his white peers in this class—and that went unrecognized and unmarked in a way that let assumptions about drugs overshadow concern for what might be happening to throw him off academically in this class. His failure was treated as expected and natural.

Layers of violence

Rahul lived in a big house at the end of a dead-end street with his dad. His mom and sister lived a couple of hours away. While he had cousins, aunts, uncles, and other family nearby, his dad traveled a lot so he was alone a lot. Khalil's mom tried to advocate for Rahul. She talked to his father and tried to help Khalil understand and find ways to support him. "You know the hard thing for Rahul," she told me, "is that he lives in this big house … but his dad is gone all the time … it's hard for him to be alone like that. He doesn't like it that his dad is gone all the time. I talked to Khalil about it one time and asked him: 'Do you think Rahul likes being in that house all by himself? How do you think it would feel? It's hard for him when his dad is gone, in Hawaii or wherever.' I know that Rahul's been having some problems at school, getting into fights or whatever, and I talked to [his dad] and he said he was going to send him away and that was really sad for me. I felt really bad about it.'

Rahul was Fijian. He strongly identified as Pacific Islander but most of the Islander students at Huerta and Westside were Tongan and Samoan and he felt like he didn't quite fit in. Tongan and Samoan families and youth were active in shaping Huerta Middle School and the city of Glenview. At the middle school, school-wide assemblies provided space for cultural celebration, dance, song, and honoring. Parents and staff with expertise, knowledge, and skill led the instruction. Students worked after school for months in preparation.

Traditional dance, re-worked and re-created in this context, functioned as a form of "survivance" (Morrill, 2016). Historically banned and punished under colonization and Christianization, the dance work enabled the memory and creation of new ways of knowing and being together under persistently annihilating conditions. Rahul didn't actively participate in Polynesian cultural celebrations at Huerta or Westside and he wasn't part of any of the Polynesian churches, youth groups, or community organizations in the area, but he was surrounded by this affirmative space while there. His family loosely practiced Hindu religious traditions (common in Fiji where indentured servitude brought many Indian people to the island) and had portraits of Hindu gods hung in the house, but Rahul did not actively talk about religion.

At the high school, many of the Polynesian students hung out at what many at school called the "Poly Wall," a space near the bathrooms where there were a few tables. One day, early in the school year, I found myself hanging out by the wall. A girl was sitting on a picnic table playing a ukulele. The sun was shining. People were talking and laughing and there was a general atmosphere of joy. About a month later, I was back again, looking for Rahul. He had punched a Tongan student, RC, during his guitar class. Khalil and their friends Fred and James told me what happened: "I saw it," Fred said, "I was there. All I heard was a pop [he made the sound by punching one fist into the other palm, his face serious] and when I turned around Rahul was all up, [he put his arms out] going 'you wanna go?' … I thought he was going to hit the teacher for a second."

Rahul's guitar teacher, a white man with earrings and a shiny bald head, sent both students to the office. "I think one kid got suspended for five days and the other one for three days. The kid who threw the punch, Rahul, I wouldn't have expected it from him. I was surprised … The other kid started saying he was a member of a gang … and he's not, so he felt like he had to do something. I remember how that was, being a boy and feeling like you had to be tough, like you had to defend yourself."

I picked Rahul up a few days after this to go to breakfast. He was suspended. We talked as I drove:

Me: Why'd you hit him?

Rahul: 'Cause he was talking hella shit and he wouldn't stop. He just wouldn't leave me alone … He just kept calling me a Norteño and shit because I wear red a lot, but I'm not. He just wouldn't stop so I hit him.

He'd gotten in another fight Saturday night with a group of Polynesian kids who were defending RC and had a cut the size of a cigarette end in his inner lip. "They all say I blindsided him. Maybe he didn't see me coming, but I didn't blindside him. You know how Polys are. They all stick together."

Me: But you, you're Fijian, aren't you Poly too?

Rahul: Yeah! And they know that, they all know I'm Poly!

Westside had no tools to help Rahul navigate the complexities of his identity—whether national, gender, ethnic, religious, racial, family, academic, city, school district, or personal. Almost all the teaching and administrative staff were white, and while Polynesian parents and staff had been an active presence at Huerta, Westside posed many of the same problems for parents as it did for students—they often felt like they were welcomed or fit only in very circumscribed ways. There was a Polynesian club, there were Polynesian celebrations as part of multi-cultural night, and football players danced the Haka (a traditional Māori dance) before games, but there was no space to wrestle with or gain deeper understanding of the complexities of the dynamics of identity structures in ways that were not centered around whiteness or a white–of color binary.

Deep work with identity, power, structures, and difference had a long history in Glenview and was core to the work community organizers and educators had done for a long time as they worked to navigate a complex, multi-cultural, multi-lingual, radically diverse space. Uhuru College, an independent college founded by Glenview organizers, was built on and engaged with global pan-African, third world, and decolonization movements. The college formed in response to the exclusion of local Black, Latinx, and Pacific Islander residents from a nearby college. But the broader educational project of thinking deeply about the interrelationship between and structural conditions facing people in Glenview as well as celebrating and honoring their ancestral diversity and knowledges had roots in the history of local organizing and global movement building that organizing was tied in to.

Ironically, Rahul's fight with RC came just as Rahul was trying to do better in school. "I've been trying," he told me. "I've been going to class and paying attention." His science and math teachers both confirmed that he had been showing up and doing his work. We talked about how the suspension was going to mess him up. "I know! I want to do my homework. I've been trying to get it from them." The vice principal had said she would call his parents to have them pick it up. "I haven't heard anything from her so I guess she didn't get it. I called my dad and told him to call her but I guess he's just too busy in Montana." I could see the hurt on his face. There was a tone in his voice, a slight undercut.

That was October. Rahul was suspended for five days. I picked up his homework from his teachers and brought it to him. The vice principal told me that his World Studies teacher didn't give any homework because Rahul had a 30 percent in the class, so what was the point. His science teacher said he was doing well. His Geometry teacher handed me a quiz on which he got a 70 and said, "He'll be happy not to have failed, that's what happens when you pay attention and do your homework." His English teacher handed me a pile with no specific instructions. His teachers' approach to Rahul's ongoing struggle was passive—they were here to teach; if he showed up to class and did his work. If he did not, it was not their problem.

The rest of the semester was quiet. Shortly before winter break Rahul began dating a girl. She was mixed Tongan, Samoan, and Fijian. I would see them cuddling together around campus, her on his lap, him holding her gently. "I'm trying to keep her," he told me. "She's like the best thing that happened to me yet. Everything else is fucking up. In school. At home."

Rahul failed Geometry and World Studies and got an FA (failure to attend) in PE. He had a C in Science, a B in English, and an A in Guitar. His grades might have been slightly better, but he was suspended once more, right before finals. He believed Mrs Cameron had missed marking a couple assignments he had completed in Geometry, but any grade corrections had to be brought to her before the final and he was suspended before he could raise his concerns. He was prepared to advocate for himself, but his persistent suspension left him isolated from means of correcting problems, jeopardizing his academics even further.

When we got back from break in January, Rahul told me, "Me and school just don't get along …. It's just, I don't know. It's not working out." I asked him what he meant, and he replied, "I don't know. I can't deal with it. I mean, I could deal with it. I could take all the work and what not. It's just all the, like, the administrative. It's just all that stuff that gets on me."

I'm a hot spot

In February, Rahul was suspended three weeks in a row. The first suspension was for smoking, the second because of how he talked to a teacher. "He just kept saying I'm irresponsible so I'm like, you know what, 'fuck this class and fuck this school!' and they suspend me for three days for that." The third was because the police, seeing him at the bus stop during school hours, had sent him to the office for a pass. When he got there, "Mr K, he just said, he said, Sharma (his last name) come into my office now. I was like, 'aw hell no, every time I go into your office, I end up getting suspended' …. So he said, 'you're suspended for four days then.' Just for that."

This was his sixth suspension of the year. He was beginning to talk about getting kicked out of the school, back to his "home school."

Like a number of Huerta students, Rahul had to petition to attend Westside. The school, while closest to his home, was not his "home school" under the desegregation plan. Without a transfer he would have been bused 45 minutes away. He wanted to stay close to friends from Huerta but his permission to be at Westside was revocable. Rahul was neck and neck with his friend Polo for most days of suspension, though he thought he had more. "I don't think no freshman has twenty-two days of suspension." His friend Manuel had been sent back to his "home school" for fighting. His friend Snoop had shown up at school to get his schedule after break and they told him he was no longer a student there. Milo was also expelled.

I asked the school principal about the suspension and expulsion policy, something for which the school had previously been subject to civil rights complaints. He talked first about the policy of sending students back to their home school. "A lot of kids from Westside really don't want to be bused that far, or at least to certain schools. Particularly to [Rahul's home school]. I don't know what it is about [that school] … I think if they had their way, they just wouldn't have kids from Glenview as all." A lot of students transferred to Westside. The school required students maintain a 2.0 average and "not get into too much trouble." He went on, "we also try to get rid of the kids who are fighting, a kid may get transferred after their third fight, or if they're really confrontational or disrespectful. So kids who are being defiant, arguing a lot with their teachers or causing disruptions. We don't suspend people for small things. We don't suspend people for truancy, but we're pretty strict on a lot of things. We have no tolerance for any kind of violence, or intimidation, or harassment, or robbery."

Of Rahul's six suspensions, only one had been for violence. The others were for smoking and defiance. Rahul and I talked about smoking. I told him "I smoked the whole time I was in high school, never got in trouble once. Just didn't smoke on campus."

He reminded me that he'd learned that lesson, but they still suspended him just for being at the bus stop

Rahul: Yeah, so I'm like, come on man, you all get me for in school and out of school. You just can't leave me alone … I'm a hot spot.

Me: A hot spot?

Rahul: Hard to miss.

Me: Hard to miss.

Rahul: And I'm so big too, so they can see me so easily.

Me: Yeah, you're hard to hide, huh?

Rahul: Yeauhh. Long ass hair just, poof, they see my big ass, see me running, they still see my hair.

And, of course, he was right. My attributing my not getting caught to my own savvy regarding where I smoked was nonsense, the kind of disregard for systemic racism that reproduces white supremacy through sloppy comparison. The data are crystal clear that students of color are disciplined, suspended, and expelled in ways and frequencies radically disproportionate to white students for the same behavior (Wun, 2014). Students of color are hyper-surveilled (Rios, 2012). They are punished more harshly (Fine and Ruglis, 2009). And they are less likely to be treated with care and concern, their full humanity invisibilized (Simmons, 2019). Rahul was a hot spot. So were most of his friends. Their status as outsiders at this school, subject to removal if they didn't comply, was clear. As, from the principal's remarks, was their lack of welcome at their "home" school. A typical semester is 75 class days. By mid-February there had been a little more than 100 days of school. Rahul had been suspended almost one quarter of those days.

The consequences of suspension for school-based learning are clear. Students lose content, lose connection to the classroom, and have a difficult time catching up from missed days (Balfanz, Byrnes, and Fox, 2014). The school-to-prison or school-to-confinement pipeline describes the relationship between students of colors' disproportionate disciplining in school settings and their disproportionate contact with and containment within the criminal justice system (Morris, 2018). Youth of color are persistently treated and perceived as adults by the criminal justice system, denied the presumption of innocence and caring often directed at white youth (Soung, 2011). All youth are subject to status crimes, punishment specifically because of their age, for things that would not be punishable for adults, such as leaving school, or smoking. Youth of color are disproportionately criminalized for these. Young people of color are imagined and treated as threats in ways that not only result in excess criminalization and punishment, but also result in their abuse and murder.

Anti-Black police violence had been a grounding concern for many of those who had fought for the incorporation of the city of Glenview. A young Black man running from police the early 1960s was shot in the back by the sheriff in Glenview while scaling a fence. This moment crystallized a set of broader concerns that motivated many residents. "The main reason we wanted to become an independent city," an elder named Lani remembered, reflecting on the organizing of the time, "was to control the police." In more recent years, Glenview had increasingly, in the face of deep resource constraints, relied on partnership with police departments from surrounding white communities, stripping that control away.

As we talked that day in February, shortly after the murder of Oscar Grant at Oakland's Fruitvale station, Rahul described a violent encounter between him and his friends and the police, fueled by racism and aggression from white "task force" officers from surrounding cities. He told me Fele and Snoop had been "locked up … police brutality." He then proceeded to explain the violence and chaos that ensued after police responded to a robbery of the "corn cart lady" who sold elotes [corn on the cob] near Huerta. One of Rahul's friends had robbed her of $8 with a fake pistol he had borrowed, then gone to McDonalds, where Rahul and his friends were. The police quickly came to McDonalds and handcuffed the young person who committed the robbery, but then one of Rahul's other friends began "playing around with the cops, pretending like he was running away from them. The cop asked him, 'you think that's funny?!' and then the crack, the cop just grabbed him by his hair and yanked him down. He resisted, 'hell no!', 'what the fuck? I didn't do nothing'!". From there everything escalated. Snoop tried to talk to the police outside and was beaten; Rahul tried to help him, but an officer pulled their baton and tried to hit him. Another friend who, egged on by an officer who said "'fuck you guys…you all want to hit me? Then hit me!'" had hit a cop who "just grabbed him by his hair." Rahul tried to pull the friend back into McDonald's, but the police "just yanked him out with him in my arms." Someone threw a rock and broke a cop's window and the police punched two more kids in the face. At the end, an officer chased down one of Rahul's friends, punched him, and told him: "If I could I'd kill every one of y'all mother fuckers over here."

By the time Rahul told me all this, everyone who had been arrested had been to court. He explained the marks on the young people's bodies from the police violence. His friend told him, "Jemar, the tall Black kid, when he was in the courtroom, his neck, you could see bruises on his neck," and Fele's mom "said [he] was all bruised up on his neck and limping. He couldn't even walk 'cause what the cops did to him the day before and so was the Samoan kid named Tea." He attributed what happened to the police being from Westside, the "task force." Glenview police, he said, wouldn't do that, "they do, all they do is their job, they do what's actually right … we never had that police brutality going on." As we drove home, I asked him about Oscar Grant, who had been murdered by police a few months prior in Oakland. "They're going to let that motherfucker out on bail. That's some shit. Say if the kid were going to shoot the police, they'd sentence him to life or execute already."

Rahul's friend terrified and robbed a woman selling corn on the cob to children right next to the school. And Rahul and his friends helped hide the fake gun. No one I knew in Glenview would have defended their actions or wanted them to go without consequences, but the police response dramatically escalated the violence. The response Rahul described, provoked by Fele's mocking attempt to run, fits within broader patterns of police, particularly white police, responding with murderous rage and brutality to perceived insults, disrespect, or lack of subservience from youth of color (Stovall, 2018). That rage and the disregard for the lives and safety of young people of color is rooted in long histories of racist policing and is deadly, dangerous, and traumatizing. White youth's actions, even when violent, harmful, destructive, and deadly are often treated as pranks, the results of trauma or mental illness, or just kids being kids. Those of youth of color, in contrast, are often responded to with extreme and overwhelming physical and juridical force.

Black and Native adolescents are six time more likely, and Latinx adolescents three times more likely, to be killed by police than white adolescents. According to the American Medical Association, nearly 16,000 young people were treated for injury after interactions with the police in California hospitals between 2005 and 2017. Black youth were by far the most injured group, but Latinx, American Indian, and multiple or other-race youth were also overrepresented. Pediatric frameworks recommend well-child questions about police interactions. Unfair stops, even without physical violence, can result in anxiety, depression, PTSD, chronic stress, diabetes, and obesity. Black, Latinx, Native American, Pacific Islander, and other groups subject to police and military violence and brutality have had to find ways to organize around, heal from, and grapple with the ongoing trauma of these encounters (Camacho, 2021).

When all this happened, Rahul had just turned 14. As he struggled with loneliness and trauma, Rahul's behavior was treated over and over again, by adults at Westside and by the police, through the lens of punishment and control. At no point was Rahul offered supportive resources—therapy, counseling, or academic support. Rahul's friends, particularly his Black friends, were expelled and incarcerated. While most Glenview youth were not pushing boundaries in the ways Rahul and his friends were, and most were not getting suspended, youth of color were dramatically over-represented in suspensions and often carried stories of brutalizing encounters with school authorities and the criminal justice system in ways radically disproportionate to or completely in disregard of their actual actions (or lack thereof). Rahul, and many of the other young people from Glenview, felt safer from this kind of state and extra-state violence when they were in Glenview. This wasn't accidental. The advocacy work of Glenview city leaders to ensure police in the city were properly trained and integrated with the community, combined with youth of color's hyper-visibility in white communities, made crossing into Westside to go to school a threatening and dangerous experience for many Glenview youth.

Rahul's afterward

When we met up years later, Rahul was going to community college, living at his dad's house, and trying to get a job. As mentioned previously, Khalil was staying there too. The driveway was packed with cars, so I had to turn sideways to get through. I entered through a polished wood door and found myself staring at plush carpets, polished wood furniture, and a staircase with a banister. Everything was spotless. We sat on fluffy sofas in a sunken living room in front of flat screen TV. Sitcoms from the 1990s were playing. On a different day I would visit the place he had created in the garage, which I called his mancave. Couches, an ashtray, a glass cabinet with bongs, a picture of the kindergarten class from Huerta, and a picture of Rahul's friend who had been shot and killed a few months back. There was a graffiti lettering paper with "Khalil" written on it that their friend who had been shot and killed, Goose, had created in 5th grade. On the wall there was a dart board, a picture of Marylin Monroe, another of Al Pacino. A green carpet covered the floor. Westside High was a distant blur for Rahul. He had been to five schools since then, before getting his GED. We mostly talked about old stories and the trauma that came with his parents' divorce and mom's, and then stepmom's, departure when he was a child. He re-told stories I had heard when he was younger. He was still friends with Jemar and Lalo. Just before we stopped talking Khalil walked in:

Rahul: Where's the biology book. Did you do this reading?

Khalil: Yeah.

Rahul: Fuck, I got to do some homework too.

I asked about his plans. He said he was feeling okay about college, "shit was pretty cool, when I went back, I was like, I felt kind of good." He was thinking of getting his associate's, "Depending. I don't know. I'm gonna see how everything pans out, I guess. I'm waiting. I'm waiting to see if I get the job with my dad. At, like, at the company he works for, 'cause if I get that … they'll pay for me to, like, go to certain classes that I need and stuff so I'll be good. They'll send me to San Diego or, like, New York and stuff and like just help train." I took a picture of him, holding my 8-month-old son, standing in the driveway. They are both smiling wide. Rahul's hair is pulled back and he's wearing a grey work shirt with a nametag stitched in it. A sticker of a goose, representing his friend who was shot, is on the car behind him.

8
Jonathan: I know everybody

Before I met Jonathan, I sat in on his double accelerated Geometry class at Valley Vista middle school. His teacher, Mr Lopez, was Filipino. He had a hand-painted poster outside his door that read Mr L. On the inside, sloppy curved rows of desks faced the center. A few couches covered in sheets were against the wall. The students were reviewing for an exam. As class began, they started firing sophisticated geometry questions at Mr L, mostly asking him to review stuff on the test but then asking things like, "So if those two angles are complementary, then those two are also?" and "Can you review how to draw parallel lines with the compass?" Again, the answers were quick and straightforward. There was not a lot of slowing down in case anyone didn't get it, and it seemed as if everyone did get it. If they didn't, they asked again. They would be taking the final tomorrow and the next day—45 questions tomorrow and 55 the day after that. I talked to Mr Lopez afterwards and he said, "Yes, they're all in eighth grade, they are double accelerated which means they are really bright and will take stats in their senior year of high school, calculus their junior year."

Jonathan hung out with Amy and her friends in the "drama group," although I didn't see them together much in eighth grade. I didn't really know him then. I met him in high school, over at Amy's lunch table. When I asked if he'd like to be part of the project, he said "maybe it would be a way for me to get some attention. You know, we have this joke, we say that because I'm Asian I blend in with the desks and so no one ever notices me." Penelope Pruitt, the Valley Vista counselor, had expressed concern about "quiet Asian kids." Jonathan wasn't quiet. Rather, as he pointed out, race shaped how he was (and was not) seen. Despite being academically and socially extroverted and gregarious, Jonathan was still invisibilized, still framed as quiet. Jonathan loved to act and was excited about the upcoming play. He was the understudy for a part in Agatha Christy's *The Mousetrap*. "It's an interesting part to play … because my character's gay. I mean, I'm not gay, but my character is and it's interesting. It's interesting to play it and just kind of experience what it might be like." Jonathan had soft eyes, a short cut hair, and was tall and thin. I wrote down the date for his play on my hand.

Like many other Valley Vista students, he had found the transition to high school really smooth and easy. He was taking a full slate of advanced classes. He did play practices after school and debate on weekends. He had been doing martial arts on the weekends but dropped because "I figured that's a bit too busy for me." He felt like he was doing okay. His parents expected him to get good grades, "you know, if I get a B+ but I get two A+'s, which is what happened the first trimester in eighth grade, then they'll let it go. They still won't be that happy about it, but it's okay … especially if it's like an 89 percent." As a result of his B+ in English, Jonathan had taken English classes over the summer to hone his skills. "Writing essays was really difficult for me in eighth grade, but Westside really helped with that, as well as the programs over the summer, but I think Westside takes its time more …. Writing more isn't necessarily writing better." Despite his appreciation for the instruction he was getting at Westside, he was still worried about his grade. "I didn't want to get a B+ in English again."

Jonathan was in AS English. His teacher, Ms Hart, was also Amy and Cam's teacher. She loved Jonathan's creativity and his passion for acting, but was a bit worried that he was too centered on grades. "Oh, he is so interesting. He got the highest score, like, on the first set of essays. So, he's got the highest score of all the ones that I graded, and I think he kind of got into a little false sense of confidence … he's so much, like you know, 'everything is the way it's got to be for a reason' and yet he totally defies this stereotype because he's got all this beautiful creativity in him, where, like, he gets up and performs … he's just so cool … he blows me away with these things sometimes and then I, and this makes me really sad because I feel like over the course of the year I've seen him kind of get more and more into the, 'I've just got to get that grade and my interaction with my teachers is going to be about making sure I get these points.'" She said he was "doing great" but "if he gets like an A- or a B+ on a paper it's just like, it kills him. I feel like I have to talk to him before he leaves the room because I don't want him feeling upset … I still always have this anxiety that somewhere in him something is saying, it's not fair, it's not fair, it's not fair."

She shared the worry of a number of school officials that some of the very "high achieving" students were being harmed by a stressful culture that the students didn't necessarily have the coping tools to handle. "I'm worried about this culture of expectations that we have here, and everything has to be the A because I feel like Cam and Amy, like, have coping skills that kind of get them through that and maybe, I don't know. I just. I feel like he's kind of going closer to that route." She worried they had lost the sense of silliness in the classroom where "we're rollin', we're totally laughing about these stories and, like, throw these ideas out there and if they're weird, then they're weird, you know, who cares." Maybe, she said, it was that the books are different, but she reflected they still "get pretty goofy with the Odyssey sometimes though, there's some pretty kinky references and we giggle about the craziness." But she felt like, as the semester went on, Jonathan was getting locked out of this joyful learning. She read it as being about his concern with grades, but there may have been other things going on as well.

Her class had been working through *Their Eyes Were Watching God*. She felt like her students were struggling to capture the African American language used in the book. At one point in the text one of the characters gives a eulogy for a mule and she thought this would be a powerful opportunity to have students get deep into the structure of the language, play with it, and thus learn to more deeply understand and respect it. She had the students work in groups to write and perform "meulogies," eulogies to a mule. These were supposed to be done in African American Vernacular English (also known as Black Language (Alim, 2004)) in ways consistent with the text. "When I did this initially," she told me, "I gave them looser guidelines" and some students "went up and basically did the exact opposite of what I had asked them to do ... they tried to use slang words thinking that it was similar to African American vernacular, so I had to pull them aside and be like, let's go over this. Have you ever seen this word in *Their Eyes Were Watching God*? What made you think this was appropriate? So, I had to do that one intervention with two students and everything else was totally fine, the other kids totally got what I was saying." She prefaced the exercise by doing "a lot of talking about the Harlem Renaissance movement and why it was so important and this idea of, like, a cultural rebirth and celebration of art and history and I talked to them about language specifically and what happens when you remove people from their homes." She wanted them to understand the language so they could understand "the jokes and the rhythm of it." This was a thoughtful teaching exercise grounded in study of Black histories and language that asked students to engage the language with respect and care.

I was in the room when Jonathan delivered his "muleogy." Jonathan was in a group with a Latinx boy with glasses named Juan and a white boy who I didn't know. Jonathan led the muleogy. He stood on a chair and in a strong booming voice began, "We are gathered here to pay tribute to our beloved donkey, but really he is best described as an ass. Now he has gone on to donkey heaven, all skin and bones." He clearly loved being up there in front of the class. His voice was strong and deep with emotion. I could hear students around me saying things like "wow" and "incredible." The other two students in his group did not say much. Juan was the dead mule and the other kid just called out random responses like "hallelujah!" in what I guess was supposed to be a bird voice (there is a crow in the scene). The class clapped enthusiastically when they were done.

Ms Hart was prepared to intervene if the humor got out of line. A few students checked with her in advance about references. She said yes to moonshine but no to cocaine, "no illegal drugs. It's not consistent with the text anyways." She helped them understand the boundaries by looking at the text itself and its language and construction. The only group she had to actively intervene with used anti-Asian stereotypes in their skit. At one point they said, "this is an Asian mule." They held a sign with an illustration of a mule that appeared to have squinty eyes. There was some clear discomfort in the room. In debriefing the skit Ms Hart asked the group about the Asian mule. "Did I hear you right?" "No, never mind," one of the group members responded. "Because if you did say that, it would have been derogatory, and I'm sure that's not what you mean to be."

Student: No, no.

Ms Hart: Because it really wouldn't be kosher to say that kind of thing.

Cam: What does kosher mean?

Ms Hart: It refers to food but in this sense it also means good.

Despite this small intervention, the moment of racist mocking was dismissed before it was even addressed—the intervention addressed the intent (what you meant) rather than impact of the actions. When I asked her about it later, she said, "that didn't even make any sense … I didn't even get the reference so I was like, I don't know if it's bad or not but I just don't get it … if you're going for the humor aspect at a racial reference I'm pretty sure it's not good, so, I pulled him aside."

Jonathan had explored his family history for his middle school biography project, and he shared some of the details with me. Jonathan was fourth generation Chinese-American. His great grandparents on his mom's side had been immigrant farmers and had died when his grandfather was 14—"his mother from tuberculosis and his father from opium addiction." His grandfather and his brothers worked in a restaurant to support themselves. His grandfather went to high school but only finished the first year before dropping out. He became a weatherman in WWII and eventually got a law degree. Jonathan's dad's parents came to the US when his dad was 17. His grandmother worked at a nearby medical company. His grandfather was disabled and did not work outside the home.

Jonathan's great grandparents likely experienced intensive, overt anti-Asian and anti-Chinese discrimination. Anti-Chinese violence, exclusion, and segregation and anti-Asian violence more generally were rampant in much of California and the nation throughout much of the nineteenth and twentieth centuries (Takaki, 2008), and continue into the present (Fortunato and McAllaster, 2021). While the experiences and realities of Asian-Americans vary extensively by migration period, time in the US, ancestral nationality, language, place of settlement, and many other factors, discrimination was and is targeted at all Asians. The targeting of specific groups was also part of the history of this area. Historically, many Japanese farmers lived and farmed chickens and flowers in Glenview but lost their land when they were interned and sent to camps during the Second World War, never to regain it. Jonathan's ancestors had fought in that war for the US, but he still faced microaggressions from those who presumed he was from elsewhere. On at least one occasion I microaggressed Jonathan. I asked Jonathan if English was his first language, a question I would have been very unlikely to ask a white student. Often when white people are asked about their race or ethnicity they will say, "Oh, I'm just American," but will expect a more specific answer from others, implying that American and white are one and the same, interchangeable (Torino et al., 2019). This is one of many subtle ways whiteness is centered in everyday ways that harm and exclude. By asking Jonathan about his language, I implied he might not be from here … an implication explicitly tied to race and racist. Talli's mother was an immigrant from Ireland, Talli was second generation, whereas Jonathan was fourth generation in the US, but I never asked Talli about her language.

Asian-Americans have long been active in addressing racism and injustice directed at their own and other communities. Chinese advocates, activists, parents, and students were leaders in some of the most important anti-segregation and language-policy related lawsuits in the state of California and nationally (Weinberg, 2009). Asian-American organizers have been central to environmental justice, anti-police brutality, arts, affirmative action, and many other struggles. A major site of recent organizing and work has been disrupting the Model Minority myth (Lee, 2009). The myth is a pernicious use of the success of some Asian students in school in ways that both undermine Asian-American students and harm other groups. It is rooted in the idea that Asian-Americans have faced discrimination and racism but thrived, therefore they are a "model" other groups can be held against. This myth undermines services, attention, and concern for Asian-American students and groups who are not doing well or who are less well served, and detracts from the negative effects of racism on Asian-Americans who do thrive in school. By naturalizing the academic successes of some Asian-American students, this myth is used in racist ways to imply other racialized groups are lazy, culturally deficient, or uninvested in education. It is used to dismiss concerns about racism and also contributes to difficulties some Asian-American students have in being acknowledged or rewarded for their academic credentials or encouraged in their academic pursuits.

I asked Jonathan how it had been being Chinese-American at Valley Vista. "Except being the minority and kind of, you know, like, not, there's no one else, really, that's Asian, except for a couple people, I don't think it was a problem. I think that racism, although it's still alive, it's not that big a deal." Jonathan expressed that he liked being Asian, not because he thought it was "superior in any way," but just because he liked being Asian. "Any other person's probably going to say that too, about their race," he told me. While Jonathan spent his time with and was comfortable around his white Westside friends, he was proud of his Chinese heritage. He shared many privileges with his white peers because of his social class and residency in Westside, and he, in many ways, participated in the same marginalization of Glenview students that Westside students did, but he and his family were also vulnerable to and had experienced racism.

Jonathan's dad had multiple advanced degrees. His mom was also a professional. They lived in an area of Westside, nearby the school, in a much more modest house than those of the white students in this project. Jonathan said that they all got along well but his mom would get "kind of frustrated when I [do] … the normal things that teenagers do, like, I guess there's a lot of things she has not yet had the opportunity to understand about teenagers." I asked what kind of thing. "Like, um, you know, if I would rather talk than eat my lunch then she doesn't understand … she wants me to start making my own lunch again. Most of the time she'll make the sandwich and then I'll get the fruit or a bottled water."

Jonathan had maintained his group of friends when he moved from Valley Vista to Westside and, like Amy and Cam, he talked about how their friend groups had expanded to include people from the other Westside middle school and some students from what he called "oddball schools"—small private schools on the same side of the freeway. At first, Jonathan seemed really confident that he knew almost all the freshman at Westside. "If you put most freshmen in a line and I went down it, I could probably name about 96 percent of them." But when I questioned, him, "you think?" He revised his analysis "actually, maybe not, 'cause I don't know many of the Latinos' names … but that's just because I really haven't been connected with them 'cause I think that although, you now, they use World Studies and other classes to try to, um, … get that kind of, uh, segregation, do away with it but it kind of, everyone segregates themselves kind of." When I asked along what lines, he said, "well, you know, I really don't see Asian people with Latinos or, I mean, I see some white people with Latinos, just because they're kind of, you know, there's no real barrier that, that separates the two but ... I don't wanna say that, you know, the countries in relation to themselves are, like, far, like, you know Asia and Latin America is far away from each other because it is but that's kind of irrelevant. It's an interesting explanation though."

Me: What about Black kids or Samoan kids? Tongan?

Jonathan: I think that, like, not really. I haven't really had a chance to talk to them, but, I bet if I did, you know, they wouldn't think it's weird, but it's just, it isn't something that you normally do, its, you know, go up to somebody that you never really talk to and just kind of stand there or say hi or something.

He speculated he'd gotten to know kids from the other Westside school because he had friends in his group who knew people from there and that was the difference.

Westside had not been Jonathan's first choice. He'd been rejected from two private schools, which he found "kind of surprising." He had shadowed at all three schools. He felt the first private school did "a good job of maintaining a good class size but still also maintaining, like, uh, the natural... air... that's necessary to learn... if there's, like, strict teachers it doesn't really work as well. I can, I tend not to work as well under pressure, or at least my work isn't as good. So they, they did a nice job of, you know, asking people to stop talking or, you know, to I guess, not swear." People talking in class was something he "recognized happened everywhere," but wished "could have been fixed." He explained how it made it uncomfortable when the class was being disciplined "because I'm the kind of person that feels like if there's someone else being yelled at or if someone's yelling at the entire class, I feel like I'm the one being yelled at, so I don't like that feeling, so I try to avoid it."

Jonathan's favorite part of high school was debate team. His eyes lit up when he talked about it. "It's pretty exciting. I think that it really gives you an opportunity to feel like …" He never finished that sentence; instead, he began telling me about his team's alternative energy plan. "Our plan is, like, sending satellites into space to gather solar power and beam it down to earth. It's kind of, you know, at first glance it sounds kind of absurd and it's supposed to happen by 2012 and it's supposed to be key to space colonization which … is the only way to avoid the apocalypse which is going to come in 2012 supposedly." Admittedly, knowing very little about debate, this was not what I expected would be happening in debate club. I (naively) thought it would entail discussing difficult issues from multiple points of view—dialogue and engagement across difference. This sounded nothing like that.

Me: So you guys have a whole scenario built up?

Jonathan: Yeah, and then, um, that used to be our advantage but now our advantage is, like, um, space based solar power … which is key to aerospace competitiveness which is key to US Primacy. Like, US leadership and stuff like that.

Me: Are you down with US primacy?

Jonathan: Um, I think US Primacy actually causes great power wars.

We kept talking ... about how "space-based solar power uses silicon and ... that competes with the computer industry." We talked about polysilicon, synthetic silicon, black polysilicon, and many other things I knew nothing about. It was fun listening to him play and have fun with the ideas. But it also worried me.

Jonathan and his friends were preparing to be world problem solvers—to take on big picture ideas and play with them imaginatively and technically, among themselves, in search of solutions. It was at once fantastically grand and terrifyingly simple. I asked him how they decided on US Primacy. "I think it's because it's really stable and because not only did we solve for hegemony, but we also solved for economy and tech spillover and also because we have, we finally found a card that's saying ... to bolster the aerospace industry, it doesn't even have to work but the tech will spill over into the aerospace industry which will avoid great power wars, I guess."

Me: How'd you solve for economics?

Jonathan: Um, I think it's an add-on. We could read it if we wanted to, but I never read it because, frankly, that's just asking to, you know, for an economy disadvantage ... you don't actually bolster the US economy therefore you don't solve for it and economic collapse leads to extinction.

Recently, debate, like many other taken-for-granted educational spaces, has come under fire for the ways whiteness shapes the debating apparatus—how its norms and procedures reproduce white supremacy (Leaders of a Beautiful Struggle, 2014; Nasser, 2022). While these arguments directly take on debate, they ultimately also address broader academic structures. The major critiques address: 1) how performance norms are set in ways that privilege those who can mobilize excess human labor, time, and material resources; 2) what is counted and included as legitimate fodder for research, knowledge, and argumentation, particularly as this is shaped by historic exclusion from spaces of academic production, like universities; and 3) the premise that non-emotionally debating two sides of an issue in a "balanced" way without interrogating the premises and relations of power embedded within the question is in itself a white supremacist, imperialist, or dominant cultural practice. As I listened to Jonathan talk debate, I was struck by how the practice was socializing him to martial volumes of evidence and his imagination towards "solving" and "debating" premises without questioning who was being included in that conversation and how, nor the limits of his own or his peers' legitimacy in serving as the leading voices on any given issue.

Jonathan's afterward

Just before I left Westside, I had the joy of watching Jonathan in his play. He was wonderful: expressive, funny, and full of joy. I thought he might want to go into theater, but he assured me he was going to be an engineer. And he was. I wasn't able to connect with Jonathan when I went back in 2017, but I learned about him from others. After graduation Jonathan went to an elite undergraduate university, then pursued his masters. He worked in a variety of tech companies. He was purportedly happy and well.

9
Elijah: The sky's not the limit

It was open mic night at the Peace Life Project (PLP), October 2017. Day was already turning to twilight as cars lined the oak studded streets. They parked tight to the edges of the packed driveways, the only sign of housing density camouflaged by suburban homes with lawns, mostly packed to the gills with multiple families. By the time I arrived, the open mic was already in full swing. As I reached the stairs to the basement, I could hear the soft rhythms of slam poetry floating up. In the basement, twelve rows of soft couches and stuffed chairs divided by an aisle stretched back from a large, unraised stage area. Elijah was on the mic as the MC, sweating and shining and smiling at the crowd as he rolled them into the next act. His co-MC in-training sat nearby at the piano he would at one point play to hush the crowd. Behind the MCs stretched a full band, mostly made up of young people I had known since they were in middle school, now the age to have graduated from college. They were Black and Latinx and Polynesian; they played saxophones, keyboards, drums, trumpets. Sprinkled among them were their band teachers, Kai and Chris, both white, playing their own instruments: Kai on Sax, Chris on guitar. The energy in the room was joyous, caring, supportive, deep, and relaxed. Everyone was clearly there because they wanted to be, and this was a space where people were ready to show up for one another, in myriad different ways.

Elijah, like the other young people in this book, attended Westside High, but I didn't meet him until I went back in 2017. We met at the Peace Life Project house. The house was ringed by a fence with slats painted in bright primary colors by members of the community and lettered vertically with messages of hope, peace, and joy. Inside, a couple of young men sat at a table studying the history of the city, part of a broader curriculum called City Beat. From the basement, the sound of a band practicing pulsed up through the floor. Elijah and I met in the back room. The walls were covered with community agreement posters, post-its written by young people, and artwork and maps drawn by local youth. Recording equipment and instruments were scattered between the desks, printers, and files. At 23 years old, Elijah was the director of youth organizing as well as an MC and hip hop artist. He explained that the building we were sitting in was owned by a community elder whose legacy was broad and deep. "This building has a long history of social justice and historically was, like, the headquarters for everything, everything positive in Glenview. Actually, the inception of Glenview … Incorporation as a city started here."

The owner of the PLP space had begun organizing when he was in college, tying community work to the organizing work he and other Black students were doing against racism on their campuses. He, like other Black, and later Latinx and Islander, residents, had worked for decades to build community and opportunities in Glenview and address racist housing, policing, and education practices. Historically, Black leaders had constructed a myriad of alternative educational spaces dedicated to providing loving, rich, Black-centered, community-centered, critical educational experiences – spaces that local schools, steeped in racist frameworks and practices and dominated by white boards and the interests of white families, could or would not provide. Building educational alternatives entailed building creative and imaginative spaces for joy, learning, and celebration for Glenview youth. Drawing on long histories of creative Black educational labor (Anderson, 1988), leaders developed schools, Saturday schools, and after-school programs in their houses. They created freedom schools and generated projects through which young people organized, researched, and storied their community. They held music and arts spaces in basements and living rooms. They founded a college! The PLP house had been the site of organizing meetings that bridged educational projects and broader community development and justice work for decades. Glenview, like many historically Black communities (Rickford, 2016), had an amazingly rich history of Afro-centric, anti-colonial, critical, multicultural educational work. And this work was not just history.

Not only, the PLP site, but scattered all across town, in seemingly ordinary looking houses, non-profits and autonomous educational projects dedicated to food justice, environmental justice, music, the arts, technology access, housing rights, poetry and writing, peace, and much more carried on this tradition. In churches, basements, and garages, working people and students gathered in their scant time off to address gentrification, eviction, displacement, school closures, and police violence, and to create, build, and imagine a different present and future.

The work was not abstract but tied to concrete, collaborative, educational struggle against the ongoing conditions faced by youth and residents of the community. Organizers, both historically and presently, were not just working alone. They connected to movements, theories, scholars, activists, and educators nationwide and globally. The civil rights, Black and Brown power, anti-colonial, third world liberation, and Indigenous rights movements all shaped and were shaped by what was happening in Glenview.

Elijah's work with the Peace Life Project (PLP) built on these legacies of critical educational projects and spaces in Glenview. Elijah juxtaposed the work he did with Glenview youth to his experiences in schools, including Westside High. "I never really took to school," he told me, "because I never really bought into the idea of the system that is school …. I wanted to do better because I wanted to appease my mother and father … but it never resonated with me." Elijah performed well on tests and actively participated but didn't submit homework, "To me it was like a series of hoops … by someone else's standard to prove you have knowledge or something." When he started at Westside, Elijah had been placed in remedial classes. "I finished Algebra by the time I was out of eighth grade, but when I got there, they put me into, like, Pre-Algebra … they tried to put me in regular English," but when he passed the first test "with flying colors" and shared his writing, "the teachers was just like, you're not supposed to be in here." They moved him to AS. But while he actively participated, he didn't turn in work, so he ended up back in regular. He described the experience of being in AS classes (he had been in three or four) as "very much culture shock every time I went into those classes. I'm not comfortable here. I don't want to be here. Like, you know, there's nobody in here that relates to me in here and if anything was related to race, they'd all look at me."

Educators in Glenwood had worked historically to implement educational models other than the transactional and racially alienating one Elijah described, building not just outside of, but within the public education system. One site for this work was Glenview High School, the historic high school on the east side of the freeway, it's burnt skeleton now buried under box stores and a shopping mall. Glenview High was part of Parkside District, and was planned before and constructed shortly after Black families began moving to Glenview. When the Parkside District Board initially drew high school attendance boundaries, they drew them such that all majority Black and racially transitioning areas would all attend Glenview High. Glenview leaders strongly objected and residents petitioned the Parkside school board on multiple occasions seeking fair and equitable attendance boundaries for the new school. Over 3,000 Glenview residents signed a petition proposing attendance boundaries that would have split Glenwood equally between two different high schools, creating integrated schools. Residents of Parkside strongly opposed the plan, writing over 200 letters in one week, many threatening to withdraw their children. The board largely capitulated, leaving only a few small slivers of the white neighborhoods in the Glenview High attendance zone. Glenview residents continued to push for integration, petitioning the federal government which wrote numerous reports, including one from the House Education and the Workforce committee which clearly described a pattern of race conscious segregation.

Glenview parents and organizers sustained pressure for desegregation and eventually, under threat of a lawsuit, the district generated a voluntary desegregation plan, making Glenview High a magnet school and investing extensive resources to lure white students. The remodeled building was state of the art and a creative, student-centered curriculum, with ample extracurriculars, was put in place. Centered in Glenwood and drawing extensively on educational traditions, leadership, and thought from Glenwood educators, the school aimed at deep integration and justice work and creative, intensively multicultural and critical pedagogy. Initially, the voluntary plan worked, and white students enrolled in Glenview, but white students expressed fears about being in a Black space. As one student declared in a local newspaper, "It felt a little strange going to such a great school like Glenview High for three years and never being able to walk off campus. It just wasn't smart for whites to go wandering around Glenview" (Archive, 3/24/1978). White enrollments dropped precipitously. As overall enrollment at Glenview High declined, some Black parents sought to get their students into other schools or districts. Black families, like all families, have varied educational visions for their children, and some were unhappy with the curriculum at Glenview High, seeking something more conservative and traditional for their students. A group organized to "jump" their students to high schools in nearby white communities by using fake addresses or having their students stay with white families. While this was a powerful form of activism, it hurt enrollments even more.

In the late 1970s, the Westside district closed Glenview High School. The loss, like those of many other Black schools in the wake of desegregation (Walker, 1996) was deeply mourned by many in Glenview. It meant a loss of community control, jobs for Black teachers, and connection at the high school level, extensive bussing for all Glenview students, and loss of a core institution for the city, which had few community centers or resources. The creative curriculum that envisioned a collaborative, student-driven, critical model of education—one that recognized and addressed the types of concerns Elijah raised about the limits of schooling, was also gone. It also symbolized the many ways integration was not a coming together on equal and committed terms, but rather a burden borne by Black students and stubbornly resisted and feared by whites, who fiercely refused desegregation except when it was clearly in their own interest (Bell, 1987).

Elijah contrasted the segregation at (integrated) Westside, to the integration at his (segregated) middle school. "In middle school I never saw, like, real differences between me and my Mexican friends and Polynesian friends, you know, I just saw them as people. Of course, I knew they were different … but we're all just people." In high school, "it was very much segregated and it was kind of orchestrated to be that." He described the racialized geographies of the school in vivid detail, and how he dealt with them by constantly staying on the move: "I was never one to stick in one area … just kind of, like, rode off and did my thing where I fit in." But he didn't necessarily understand it all: "Race and things like that were, you know, kind of put in my face," but at first, "things were happening to me and I didn't even realize that's what they were." By his Junior year he was "coming up against it so much" he started to push back, "whenever the white kids asked me why I did something … I'd just be like 'oh, it's 'cause

I'm Black' ... I used to say it so much that they would get mad, 'you're racist!' ... it made people uncomfortable ... like, 'why you uncomfortable?'" Because of colorblind frameworks, white students often confuse resistance to racism, or critique of racism, with racism itself. Uncomfortable with being reminded, however gently, of the racist context they were in and their place in it, they dealt with discomfort by calling Elijah racist.

Colorblind language and frameworks are one way civil rights language is appropriated towards perpetuating racial inequality and undermining racial justice work. The use of "desegregation" to pursue white interest is another. Since Glenview High School was closed, three different majority-white neighborhoods had successfully "de-annexed" (transferred) their neighborhoods from Glenview Elementary School District to Parkside Elementary School District. Despite these neighborhoods having historically been active in resisting high school integration, they now used arguments for "desegregation" to their own advantage to flee a majority-Black and Brown district and boost their property values in the process. School officials and residents in Glenview immediately recognized such moves as white flight, but Westside officials insisted they are actually "integration". These neighborhoods represented the small handful of white-majority spaces that were part of Glenview district. In each case, most white children in the neighborhood (493 of 500 in the case of the first community to annex, The Alders), had already fled the district and been enrolled in private schools or transferred. As these were the most diverse neighborhoods in Parkside, residents were able to argue their inclusion in Parkside district would boost the diversity of that district with minimal impact on Glenview (as their children were already not enrolled). Derek Bell calls this type of cynical support for racial justice "interest convergence," arguing that white people have largely only supported desegregation and other efforts when they see them as in their own best interest.

Glenview residents had long fought for racial integration. They had moved into white neighborhoods, endured violence and humiliation, sought to change district boundaries, filed reports, sued, tried again, written petitions, written letters, protested, and so forth. White residents fled Black and Brown districts, resisted and refused integration, yet pursued "desegregation" when it would boost their property values, put them in a "better" majority white schools. As desegregation came to signal more and more dispossession—of critical curricula, spaces of culturally and politically responsive learning, parts of the school district, schools, attendance, jobs, etc., more and more Glenview educators began to look for other paths, refusing cynical "desegregation" projects that would result in losses for Glenview. As many did nationwide, many Black educators in Glenview looked toward sovereignty, Black nationalism, and autonomy (Hughey, 2007) with the goal of creating thriving and self-sustaining, Black-centered, community-centered educational institutions in Glenwood that could resist the persistent appropriation, dispossession, and cultural and political violence youth, educators, and communities were experiencing. These movements were rooted in long traditions of Black educational thought that question the capacity of white institutions, built on and steeped in refusal of Black life, space, thought, and control, to educate Black youth (Marucci, 2017). For centuries, Black educational theorists, thinkers, scholars, and practitioners have grappled with, debated, and pursued a wide range of creative strategies to sustain Black knowledge and pursue educational work under persistently, systemically, violent conditions (Givens, 2021). The strategies have varied widely, from very rigid and conservative to progressive and critical models, from integration, to self-help, to Black Power. What these movements have shared is an overwhelming commitment to the excellence, brilliance, and inherent worth and value of Black children, Black thought, and Black people and a recognition that these commitments are systemically lacking. This struggle has been and is unrelenting, as is the structural, institutional, interpersonal, and educational white violence Black educational movements work to contest, combat and address.

One of Elijah's deepest frustrations with Glenwood and Parkside, was that his counselors had never connected him to the arts. "To this day they don't even hook kids from the hood up with resources that will help them move on or even try to figure out what is going to help this child be successful." He felt like if he'd found a jazz band earlier, he "mighta been a little more grounded ... passed all my classes." Elijah graduated with a 1.7 GPA; "I don't buy into the structure that they try to put to your intelligence ... I understand complex ideas and my brain doesn't just operate on some mundane level, but if you looked at my GPA from high school you might think ... I couldn't read or shit." On the contrary, he was the fastest reader in his class. "Reading was my pastime. The library knew me. The librarians knew me. They would hook me up with books. They would tell me when the next Harry Potter was dropping." Elijah's critique of schooling didn't stop at the performance, gatekeeping, and fakeness of it. He saw it as tied to capitalism, to structures of inequality, to a system perpetuating injustice. GPA, he said, "is just a matter of how hard you will work … to appease this system." Through his work with PLP, he had started thinking concretely about systemic injustice. In their study circles he had begun to "really dive into and think about the complexity of the system and how it connects to people buying into a belief." "I didn't have the tools or the understanding to really articulate it that way until recently," he reflected. When I was younger I knew about the arts … and I couldn't even articulate it, that this was, like, 'arts,' … I just knew I liked to sing and dance in front of people and make them all feel good … spread a message through, you know, song and stuff like that."

He had gotten into music through his church. He would sit and watch the music section play and then "one day somebody told me that I could switch off and play for them. It was, like, in the middle of church and he was like, here, you can play." But at Westside, he didn't realize he could access the music program until his junior year, at which point he started in freshman band. "I was like 17, 16, playing with 13- and 14-year-olds … I jumped in the game so late, you know, like why can't people tell me about things earlier!" This wasn't just about the high school, Elijah clarified. "I didn't know about it because my school didn't provide me with it, you feel me? But Valley Vista … and all those other schools … they all had music programs. I didn't know what a music teacher was or what he even taught, you know! And that all came from a lack of funding for music and the arts. What's the first thing to get cut … No Child Left Behind, that just meant 'cut funding.' That's all it meant … No Child Left Behind … you left them all. All of them. Every single one. They're all worse off." Despite all the critical educational labor in Glenview, the resource gaps were extreme, test scores reflected the profoundly difficult circumstance families and the schools and district were attempting to navigate, and a "no excuses"/ "accountability" policy landscape meant district like Glenwood, faced with overwhelming challenges, were blamed, gutted, and penalized. Among the first programs to go in the effort to concentrate scarce resources where they would raise test scores, were the arts (Lipman, 2011).

While Elijah experienced racism and culture shock at the high school, there weren't a lot of tools to help him make sense of it. He wasn't oblivious to race, "I definitely knew what race was … when you grow up Black you have to … when you grow up any color except white … you have to know what race means." But he didn't know "how much to keep in mind, like, the differences when interacting." There were a couple of spaces that helped him process his experiences. There was a "PhD Black dude" that taught a group for Black students. They would come to a room to read and learn about Black culture and do homework. "He kind of gave me some tools, gave me, um, knowledge about myself … about my history and stuff like that … he was one of the only people on campus who I felt cared about, you know, my success." In Elijah's senior year he had a creative writing teacher whom he also loved. "She was pretty dope."

Black students, families, and teachers had been organizing for four decades against the harassment, lack of teachers of color, and culturally negligent curriculum they experienced at this and other Westside schools. Mrs. Washington, the school's only current Black teacher, explained that when she first came in the late 1960's, she was part of a cohort of Black teachers recruited from across the country in response to protests from Black students, families, and organizers. "People felt that there's wasn't Black literature and things like that withing the school, that they needed more teachers who could, you know…be able to speak to those types of things, those type of situations, just more equality, more rights." She described her own educational experience, "I went to high school back in Baltimore. You were put in the back of the classroom and you fended for yourself…teachers didn't, there were teachers that didn't teach you, that felt you were ignorant and couldn't do anything." Her school had automatically tracked her to be a secretary, "I had to literally tell my parents and them that I wanted to be in the academic program and I wanted to go to college." She connected through the fact that she had to keep "fighting and fighting" to be "put into that curriculum." "I don't know if that in essence was what was going on here, but the African American students just wanted to be heard and they wanted to be given equal chance and they wanted to say hey, I want to go to college too, I want to get the same type courses too." Of the nine African American teachers recruited at that time, she was the only one who remained. She talked about how lonely that was on a personal level and how it harmed the students "that's one of the things that is missing, because I think those students deserve teachers that they can look up to and say hey, I can." Despite decades of advocacy, the school continued to offer no courses in Black history, had only one Black teacher, and persistently failed to adequately advise, support, and counsel Black students. Mr. Larson, a bilingual resource teacher, reiterated reasons given by many teachers, "the principal here is sort of a political position in a lot of ways…it's keeping a constituency happy in a lot of ways...that's got to be difficult...to make the school what the affluent community wants it to be as opposed to making it a public school that serves everyone...a lot of political pressure comes from one end of that spectrum."

As Elijah got involved with Glenview programs, he started performing at open mic nights at the Ocean Street program run by Talli's friend Mele's parents, and also began working with youth in schools through the Art Wall Program. He came to family nights at PLP where "basically, young folks from Glenview would get together and they would teach us … and they would feed us." As his arts and leadership work grew, Elijah was hired to lead a "youth driven action team" focused on designing an arts center in Glenview. He worked with 10 or so young people. "I would have them … do reflective work … would invite people to come do small things to teach them things and then also we planned and executed community events." They worked on a block party, music festival, and performances to highlight local artists." Elijah and his youth team had been working with architects, consultants, branding experts, Lynch maps, urban development scholars, Environmental Impact Reports, traffic flows, and interviewing residents. They were trying to make the arts center a deeply community-centered project: "We have been inviting the community out for the architects to glean information and go back with something that actually is based on the community input, and not just ours, and bring that back with the community, show them … eventually you get to a point where the community feels really good about … the design and the direction."

Elijah wasn't sure if he was the "best person" or the "worst person" for this work, but "if it's my responsibility, then it needs to get done. I know that kids love me … we were all kids, and I knew that, you know, people naturally gravitated towards my leadership, mostly because I don't see myself as a leader." Elijah contrasted his own pedagogy to that of the schools. "I have a natural inclination towards collaboration rather than dictatorship … I don't just … tell people how it's gonna go … 'cause I know at the end of the day, when people are able to own something, it goes further." That, he said, is "the big thing with education, too, it's like, you know, teachers don't give students the opportunity to own their knowledge, own their education, own what they learn. It's like, do it the way I'm teaching you and shut up." Elijah didn't use "'teacher mode.' I ask questions because I don't want people to feel like I'm just telling them what to do." I had watched Elijah teach music and seen his pedagogy in action. I tried to summarize what I'd seen for him: "There's just this way in which, like, there's this back and forth and growing. I don't know. It was really neat to watch. It was beautiful."

But this work was not without vulnerability, "I can still lose my job today … they're not going to write me down as a founder." He wasn't sure whether he had passed on a possible career as an artist, if he might have been better off somewhere else, "because this is where all my marbles are. Like this is where all of my … I don't even got nothing to fall back on, you know what I mean? Like, I've put all of my energy, all of my strength, spirit, and knowledge into this. All of who I was … I don't have a fallback plan. I don't have a BA or an MA or anything. All my experience is working with youth, working with non-profits … and unless BET (Black Entertainment Television) is going to hire me every year, I'm going to need to find other jobs."

A few years prior, Elijah's family had been displaced from the home he grew up in when the landlord sold the house. His mom died a month later. He was still reeling from the loss, writing songs to her, holding space for her. He felt that through "genetics and osmosis and spirit, like, the next generation will feel your experience … like elephants, they have like generational knowledge, so like if a baby gets lost at a young age, it could eventually find its way back to the herd … most of it is unconscious and untappable … so, like, I feel like in some way or another, she still feels, you know, she still sees what I see." Elijah talked about other things he carried from his mom, like his radical imagination, to "break through the sky." "I feel," he said, "like people of color get to a certain point and always feel like it's, like we can't go further …. It just feels like there's ten million hoops to jump through to get to the next level … something don't click … don't move over … doesn't give us access … it's like, the sky's the limit, while everyone else is like on Saturn, Mars, Jupiter. Like chillin'. Looking down on earth …. Everyone's looking at the sky and being so wishful and hopeful to make it there. Like you can go past there and like you can go forever, for miles and miles and if you can't manage to get to the next planet and you die … your offspring or whoever else comes after you can take the ship and get there … like the sky isn't, the sky isn't the limit … like flight is, like, impossible for humans. We have to build machines to get there. But somebody, all the fuck they wanted to do was fly. And so they built a machine to help them do it and that's what they did. That's what you gotta do …. Somebody flew."

In addition to the art center work, Peace Life Project had been involved for a long time in organizing to fight eviction and gentrification. Their I Heart Glenview campaign, grounded in the message "this is my home" countered the tunnel vision from over the bridge, which saw Glenview primarily through the lens of violence and lack. In August 2016, a group of Glenview youth held signs while panelists talked about the housing crisis in a bookstore in Westside. "This is our home," "Thumbs down to displacement," "Glenview is not for sale," "community is priceless," read their signs, some adorned with glitter, one painted with a stop sign, the "o" on "our" lined with stick figures holding hands. In April 2015, residents and youth marched against gentrification, holding signs that read "Stand up Glenview: Black power, Brown power, Poly power." Youth from Huerta made signs adorned with spray painted fists above "Glenview," wore shirts that said "hope dealer," and carried signs that read "Glenview is our Home: No Displacement." These manifestations of love and labor represented years of work on the part of Glenview youth and their allies to counter the negative messaging about this city spread by schools, representatives, the press, neighbors, and general word of mouth.

Despite studying racism in these communities for years, it took me much longer to see the deep knowledge work, organizing, joy, justice, and labor of Glenview youth families and organizers, and its long history. Intoxicated with this resistance work, I began thinking I would write a book titled *I Heart Glenview*; a book about the creative labor of youth and families fighting for their community, their education, and one another. When I proposed this idea to Miguel, a community activist fighting evictions, he was appalled. "What do the youth do???!!!" he repeated my question back to me incredulously. "What they do is suffer!!!" He would not allow me to romanticize youth activism over the systemic violence that provoked it and the death-dealing damage this violence caused—whether in the schools or the community. I met Miguel at a city council meeting where families were protesting the city's crackdown on code enforcement. The city was evicting people from converted sheds and other backyard dwellings it considered safety hazards and code violations, after a previous moratorium elapsed. They were sending teams of police and city representatives, giving ten-day notices.

I had arrived at the Glenview city council chambers early and wandered around the library. Moms and grandmas sat on couches with young people, community volunteers were helping with homework, kids played on colorful mats in the children's area. It was already getting dark outside. People—mostly Latinx, but also Black, white, Asian, and Pacific Islander—began to trickle into the council chambers. A nun dressed in a blue sweater was helping translate for a man looking at the handouts, considering filling out a speaker card. Within a few minutes the room was packed. As the meeting began, family members, clearly nervous, clutched small red paper signs that read "stop the evictions." They took to the mic one by one, thanked the city for putting them on the agenda, for considering their words, and briefly explained that they were worried about how they had been treated, about losing their homes, about having nowhere to go: "Good evening, I've lived in Glenview for the past 27 years and my motivation for being here this evening is to ask for a stop to the displacement of our families;" "good evening … I have lived here from 1976 … I have six children, I'm a citizen, I've given you my vote;" "Glenview is a wonderful place with wonderful people who have been here for a long time and who love it .... The wealthy people moving in ... the poor that have been here, the humble people who have been her for a long time;" "We learn in this country that we love our animals and our pets and we treat them with so much respect and I don't understand why they treat us, who are people, with less respect." Miguel was not being evicted himself but spoke on behalf of families, confronting council members: "There is a crisis going on in Glenview! What you still don't understand is that you are kicking people onto the street, children, to live in cars, supposedly to protect them!" Others spoke of the families now sleeping in the YMCA parking lot and the church parking lots.

As this comment session wrapped up, the group of 30 or so people who had come to speak on this issue filed out. The vice mayor came out and apologized for not having any translation, or even an agenda in Spanish. One of the organizers gathered everyone's attention. "Good job everyone! We got them to put it on the agenda, that's great!" I began talking to Miguel, and he told me: "*Ya no hay nada que se puede hacer en Glenview, Glenview ya se va ... tienen que explicar este a la gente ... estan pensando que ya con el moratorio ... pueden seguir viviendo pero no va a pasar.*" ("There's nothing left to do in Glenview, Glenview's already gone. This is, this a moratorium, but it doesn't do anything, they have to explain that to the people ... because they're thinking that with the moratorium, they can keep living here, but it's not going to happen.")

I met later that week with Elijah. I expected him to embrace this organizing; instead, he sided with the city. "To be honest with you, code enforcement, they been working on that for, like, years.

And it's probably, like, unethical how they're being kicked out, but they did give them ample time to bring those up to code, like two years …. A garage can be converted but a shed, like the shed in my backyard, can't be converted with water, electricity, and gas running through it. Really? That's the issue. It's like, you don't just have someone living in the back and taking showers in the house. You convert the back tool shed to a living-quarters. It's not gonna work like that. A stove, and lights, electricity in, like, a ten-foot box. Like, you know, that's just, like, the worst. It's like, we, it could flood and we all get electrocuted. The gas could leak and we could all get blown up. Just like that. Boom."

PLP helped organize for the first moratorium, that which had granted two years for landlords to fix substandard and not-to-code dwellings, but no amount of delay was going to fix the fact that people could not afford to live in this city; could not afford to live in anything more than a converted shed or their car. This is what families kept fighting and fighting and fighting for: to not get kicked out of a shed someone had hotwired with electric and gas and fed a water line to. Glenview educators were similarly working to sustain schools hotwired together amidst massive resource gaps, continually under the threat of school closure, supporting students and families facing seemingly endless displacement and eviction. They were often overwhelmed and children, despite all their creative resistance, survival, and love, suffered, in profound ways, in the face of these resource gaps. These conditions were not accidental or incidental but a result of explicit policy decisions, resource hoarding, and white and wealthy refusal locally and nationally. Elijah sings, "I love this town but it ain't right …"

Conclusions: Education, abolition, segregation, dispossession, decoloniality

Glenview educators, families, and young people have never relied on one single path or vision in the struggle for educational justice. They have pursued a wide range of tactics, strategies, theories, networks, movements, projects, and everyday actions as they have worked to carve out space amidst white supremacist, capitalist, and colonial violence. Building, imagining, visioning, reimagining, and re-storying the city has been one of those projects. Refusing segregation and insisting on space, resources, and access has been another. Refusing annihilation, appropriation, occupation, resource loss and annexation is yet another. As I have tried to convey through the accounts of five Glenview youth and their families, the everyday work that young people did—fighting for their languages, knowledges, and communities to be respected; defending one another and their families; persisting with schooling towards their own ends; and refusing schooling when it became too dehumanizing—is also, centrally, part of this struggle. Glenview residents and youth were constantly creating and recreating, finding ways to construct space, language, pathways, resources, supports, selves, community, and pride under systematically annihilating conditions. Even as they created, their new creations became, in turn, new targets for dispossession as corporate landlords continued to evict, and educational reforms targeted their schools for closure.

Westside youth began to participate in the logics of white supremacy long before they had any tools to critically reflect on them. Histories of their community's resource hording, refusal of racial justice, and pursuit of "pure white spaces" (Paperson, 2010) were occluded from them. Raised on stories of colonial adventure, up-by-your-bootstraps success, and their community's own benevolence, they were neither pushed nor asked to think critically about their own identities, resources, violences, or the conditions in which they were enmeshed. The work they did (if any) towards deepening their racial literacy, they largely did on their own, aided by Glenview youth who pushed back on and challenged them. Westside youth did learn about struggles for racial justice elsewhere (such as South Africa), but these were disconnected from their lives. The white adults in their lives regularly signaled that racism happened long ago, somewhere else, and was done by other people. If they had any relationship to racism, it was to critique from a distance, not be accountable in the present. Invested in their own and their community's "goodness," often when opportunities did arise to engage with Glenview, white students did so in the role of helper, mentor, or teacher—roles often central to the benevolent violence of empire (Kēhaulani, 2022). But they also engaged through friendships and chided against the contradictions they saw, were frustrated with their own awkwardness and incompetence, and longed for deeper understanding. Of course, for young people from Westside like Jonathan, whose family did experience racism—presently and historically—but who also shared some kinds of class privilege and proximity to whiteness, this was complex. All identities are complex, multiple, and layered, but the underlying structural dynamics of these contexts are rooted in racist laws, economic policies, histories, histories ideologies, and practices.

The teachers at all three schools were committed to their work, invested long hours, and worked to constantly improve their teaching. Pressure to dismantle tracking at Parkside came from teachers and many had commitments to critical, multicultural, teaching. They were working with the frameworks they were trained, supported, and mentored into, most having been raised and educated in white-centric spaces. The political and economic pressure from white parents and protection of elite self-interest at both Parkside Middle and Parkside High, as well as broader political-educational landscape worked against critically engaging with the racial histories and present students were living. Most teacher education programs do not require serious extended work in ethnic studies, critical white studies, or understanding of legacies of Black, Brown, and Indigenous educational thought, movements and histories. Movements for ethnic studies in schools face political censorship and intense backlash nationwide. Educational leadership in Glenview, despite enormous resource deficiencies, worked very hard to train and support educators to be culturally, politically and economically responsive to the needs of the very diverse young people of Glenwood. Drawing on a long history of BIPOC local educational leadership, intentional and difficult multi-racial organizing and coalition building, and interwoven struggle for educational and community justice, leaders continued to work, plan, and build toward an educational otherwise, one in which the needs of BIPOC and high-poverty students were centered and students and their families were treated with love, care, respect, and excellence.

Memo's insight that Westside High School was "for the white kids" was prescient; but really, it might be argued that, despite the long struggle for educational justice, all three schools were "for the white kids." The systemic stripping and siphoning of resources, languages, knowledges, relationships, land, and so on from Black, Brown, and Indigenous communities, and dispossession of BIPOC-led and -centered schools, spaces, and projects has served to mark "good" education as white. Just as the persistence of systemic white supremacy in the social, curricular, disciplinary, and pedagogical apparatuses of schools flush with resources marks "good" students and classes as white. The marking of Glenview students, languages, histories, classrooms, spaces, city, and schools as "bad" meant these things could be erased (or closed or eradicated) and this could be understood, in dominant frameworks, as "progress." Ongoing school closures, gentrification, and the "getting out" of Glenview spaces and relationships were all imagined within frontier logics of "development"—not as displacement or dispossession, but as integration, as improvement. Meanwhile, the everyday work, value, and knowledge of Glenview students, educators, families, and community were devalued and discounted.

Work towards an educational otherwise is constant, ongoing, and persistent. Like the historic (and present) work in Glenview, it is neither uni-faceted nor uni-directional. And, like that work, it is connected to local and global movements for other kinds of justice—housing, immigration, land rights, environmental, economic, and food justice, sovereignty, abolition, and decoloniality. These struggles are at once grounded in place and nationally and globally networked—theorized and imagined from within and without. Public schools remain key sites of struggle, not just as pedagogical spaces, space of teaching and learning, but as collective community resources, a kind of commons. Collective autonomous educational projects—the kind of educational work that happens in movement building— and efforts to desegregate schools, address resource distribution, prevent school closure, and arrest resource loss are all part of this struggle. Education that is "with us," in Jaqueline's words, should work to dismantle white educational spaces, whether those be curricula steeped in white mythology, ideologies of meritocracy, or constructs of "smartness" and "goodness" tied to resource hoarding and dispossession. Dismantling "pure white spaces" constructed in opposition to and through expulsion of a ghettoized other— whether those be tracked classes, specially zoned neighborhoods, or occupied Indigenous lands—is a core part of this work; but this has to be done in ways that are not at the cost of Black, Brown, and Indigenous youth, communities, spaces, and lives.

Being "with us" also just means being present; not with Glenview residents and Glenview youth as a site of lack or site of resistance, but as contradictory, complex, vulnerable, powerful, frightened, brave, curious, thoughtful, creative people doing incredibly hard work in ways that don't always look pretty and that often feel absolutely awful; work they shouldn't have to do; work that injustice makes necessary. This often includes the work of seeking out education and trying to avoid "spirit murder" (Love, 2019) amidst unjust and dehumanizing conditions. Being "with us" means honoring, learning about, and humbling oneself to the long, complex, and entangled histories upon which this work builds—including the knowledge and experience of Glenview educators, organizers, and community members. Being 'with us' means recognizing the labor invested in staving off and surviving displacement (in multiple, overlapping, contexts), but also in producing and creating not just livable space, but pedagogical space – space, where, in the words of one Glenwood student 'the echo can be heard.' Being "with us" means doing that place-making labor while making space for joy, celebration, mourning, and contradiction. For educators, one place to start is with local histories and local struggles over place, as seen through the work of youth, activists, families, and educators who have worked toward educational justice and against the logics of displacement, (de)segregation, and dispossession.

Notes

Introduction

1. Federal 21st Century Community Learning Center funding allowed the district to contract privately run after-school programs that included limited offerings in music and art for students enrolled in the after-school program.
2. The city boundaries and school district boundaries of Glenview and Westside do not overlap. Glenview School District encompasses the eastern portion of Westside, which is similar, demographically, to Glenview City.
3. More affirming and inclusive language, such as dual language learner or emerging bilingual, is used now, but this was the language at the time.
4. Note that just as Glenview was made up of demographically similar pieces of two different cities, so was Westside. The part of Westside Talli and Amy lived in was a separate small city, overwhelmingly white and wealthy, that was part of the Westside school district.

Chapter 2: Jaqueline: It's nice but not for us

1. Fifteenth birthdays are significant in many Latinx cultures and communities. They are celebrated as "coming of age" events accompanied often by large parties, a church service, and a series of rituals including traditional dances with family and loved ones.

References

Abrego, L. J. (2014). *Sacrificing Families: Navigating Laws, Labor, and Love Across Borders.* Stanford, CA: Stanford University Press.

Abrego, L. J. & Negrón-Gonzales, G. eds., (2020). *We are Not Dreamers: Undocumented Scholars Theorize Undocumented Life in the United States.* Durcham, NC: Duke University Press.

Acuña, R. (2014). *Occupied America: A History of Chicanos.* 8th ed. Hoboken, NJ: Pearson.

Alexander, M. (2012). *The New Jim Crow: Mass Incarceration in an Age of Colorblindness.* Revised Edition. New York, NY: The New Press.

Alim, H. S. (2004). Hearing what's not Said and Missing what is: Black Language in White Public Space. In: S. F. Kiesling and C. B. Paulston, eds., *Intercultural Discourse and Communication: The Essential Readings.* Malden, MA: Blackwell Publishing, pp. 180–197.

Anderson, J. D. (1988). *The Education of Blacks in the South, 1860-1935.* Chapel Hill: NC; University of North Carolina Press.

Applebaum, B. (2010). Being White, Being Good: White Complicity, White Moral Responsibility, and Social Justice Pedagogy.

Baldwin, J. (1984). "On Being 'White'…and Other Lies." In: D. Roediger, ed., *Black on White: Black Writers on What it Means to be White.* New York, NY: Schocken Books, pp. 177–180.

Balfanz, R., Byrnes, V., and Fox, J. (2014). Sent Home and Put Off-Track: The Antecedents, Disproportionalities, and Consequences of Being Suspended in Ninth Grade. *Journal of Applied Research on Children: Informing Policy for Children at Risk,* 5(2), pp. 1–19.

Banks, J. A. (2004). Remembering Brown: Silence, Loss, Rage and Hope. *Multicultural Perspectives*, 6(4), pp. 6–8.

Bauer, N. K. (2021). What's Love got to do With it? Toward a Theory of Benevolent Whiteness in Education. *The Urban Review*, 53, pp. 641–658.

Beauboeuf-Latontant, T. (2002). A Womanist Experience of Caring: Understanding the Pedagogy of Exemplary Black Women Teachers. *The Urban Review: Issues and Ideas in Public Education*, 35(1), pp. 71–86.

Bell, D. (1987). *And We are not Saved: The Elusive Quest for Racial Justice*. New York, NY: Basic Books.

Bonilla-Silva, E. (2006). *Racism Without Racists: Color-blind Racism and the Persistence of Racial Inequality in the United States*. New York, NY: Rowman and Littlefield.

Cabrera, N. L. and Corces-Zimmerman, C. (2017). An Unexamined Life: White Male Racial Ignorance and the Agony of Education for Students of Color. *Equity & Excellence in Education*, 50(3), p. 300–315.

Cacho, L. M. (2012). *Social Death: Racialized Rightlessness and the Criminalization of the Unprotected*. New York, NY: New York University Press.

Camacho, K. (2021). *Reppin': Pacific Islander Youth and Native Justice*. Seattle, WA: University of Howard Press.

Cardinale, K., Carnoy, M., and Stein, S.J. (1998, June). *Bilingual Education: How do Local Interests and Resources Shape Pedagogical Practices?* [Report]. Stanford, CA: PACE: Policy Analysis for California Education, Stanford Graduate School of Education. Available at: https://edpolicyinca.org/publications/bilingual-education. [Accessed Oct. 3, 2022].

DeGenova, N. (2002). Migrant Illegality and Deportability in Everyday Life. *Annual Review of Anthropology*, 31, pp. 419–47.

Desmond, M. (2016). *Evicted: Poverty and Profit in the American City*. New York: Broadway Books.

Dettlaff, A. J. and Boyd, R. (2021). Racial Disproportionality and Disparities in the Child Welfare System: Why Do They Exist, and What Can Be Done to Address Them? *The Annals of the American Academy of Political and Social Science*, 692(1). Available at: https://journals.sagepub.com/doi/full/10.1177/0002716220980329#:~:text=While%20racial%20disproportionality%20refers%20to,in%20the%20child%20welfare%20system.

DiAngelo, R. (2012). *What Does it Mean to be White? Developing White Racial Literacy*. New York, NY: Peter Lang.

Dreby, J. (2010). *Divided by Borders: Mexican Migrants and Their Children*. Berkeley, CA: University of California Press.

Dumas, M. J. (2016). Against the Dark: Antiblackness in Education Policy and Discourse. *Theory Into Practice*, 55, pp. 11–19.

Dumas, M. J. and Ross, K. M. (2016). 'Be Real Black for Me': Imagining BlackCrit in Education. *Urban Education*, 514, pp. 415–442.

El-Haj, T. R. A. (2006). Race, Politics, and Arab American Youth: Shifting Frameworks for Conceptualizing Educational Equity. *Education Policy*, 20, pp. 13–34.

Fabricant, M. and Fine, M. (2012). *Charter Schools and the Corporate Makeover of Public Education: What's at Stake?* New York, NY: Teacher College Press.

Ferguson, A. A. (1995). *Bad Boys: Public Schools in the Making of Black Masculinity*. Ann Arbor, MI: University of Michigan Press.

Fine, M. and Ruglis, J. (2009). Circuits and Consequences of Dispossession: The Realignment of the Public Sphere for U.S. Youth. *Transforming Anthropology*, 17(1), pp. 20–33.

Fortunato, P. and McAllaster, G. (2021). *Addressing Asian and Pacific Islander (AAPI) Discrimination and Violence*. [Blog] Rowan

University DEI Blog. Available at: https://sites.rowan.educ/diversity-equity-inclusion/blog/2021/03/addressing-asian-and-pacific-islander-discrimination-and-violence.html [Accessed Oct. 1, 2022].

Fryer Jr., R. G. and Torelli, P. (2022). An Empirical Analysis of 'Acting white.' *Journal of Public Economics*, 94(5-6), pp. 380–396.

Fullilove, M. T. (2004). *Root Shock: How Tearing up City Neighborhoods Hurts America and What We Can Do About It*. New York, NY: Random House.

Givens, J. R. (2021). *Fugitive Pedagogy: Carter G. Woodson and the Art of Black Teaching*. Cambridge, MA: Harvard University Press.

Glicken, M. D. and Miller, R. L. (1992). Promoting Academic Achievement and Racial Understanding: Strategies for Creative Programming to Help Resolve the Dilemmas of Integrated Education. *Mid-American Review of Sociology*, XVII(1), pp. 17–30.

Gould, S. J. (1996). *The Mismeasure of Man*. New York, NY: W. W. Norton & Company.

Grady, C. (2020). Why the Term "BIPOC" is so Complicated, Explained by Linguists." Vox, June 30, Retrieved Sept. 18, 2022 from: https://www.vox.com/2020/6/30/21300294/bipoc-what-does-it-mean-critical-race-linguistics-jonathan-rosa-deandra-miles-hercules

Grande, S. (2018). Refusing the University. In, E. Tuck and W. Yang, eds., *Toward What Justice? Describing Diverse Dreams of Justice in Education*. New York, NY: Routledge, pp. 47–65.

Grosfoguel, R. (2005). The Implications of Subaltern Epistemologies for Global Capitalism: Transmodernity, Border Thinking, and Coloniality. In: R. P. Appelbaum and W. I Robinson, eds., *Critical Globalization Studies*. New York, NY: Routledge, pp. 283–292.

Harvey, D. (2005). *The New Imperialism*. New York, NY: Oxford University Press.

Hagerman, M. A. (2018). *White Kids: Growing Up With Privilege in a Racially Divided America*. New York, NY: New York University Press.

Hill, J. H. (1999). Language, Race, and White Public Space. *American Anthropologist,* 100(3), pp. 680–689.

hooks, b (1997). *Yearning: Race, Gender, and Cultural Politics*. Boston, MA: South End Press.

HoSang, D. M. (2010). *Racial Propositions: Ballot Initiatives and the Making of Postwar California*. Berkeley, CA: University of California Press.

Hughey, M. W. (2007). The Pedagogy of Huey P. Newton: Critical Reflections on Education in his Writings and Speeches. *Journal of Black Studies, 38*(2), 209–231.

Hurtado, A. L. (1988). *Indian Survival on the California Frontier*. New Haven, CT: Yale University Press.

Irizarry, J. G. and Rosa, J. (2015). Complicating Black and Brown Solidarity: Racial Positioning and Repositioning in "Post-Racial America." In: K. Fasching-Varner and N. D. Hartlep, eds., *The Assault on Communities of Color: Exploring the Realities of Race-Based Violence*. Lanham, MD: Rowman & Littlefield, pp. 13–18.

Kēhaulani, N. B. (2022). *Tender Violence in US Schools: Benevolent Whiteness and the Dangers of Heroic White Womanhood*. New York, NY: Routledge.

Kohli, R. and Pizarro, M. (2022). The Layered Toll of Racism in Teacher Education on Teacher Educators of Color. AERA Open, 8(1), pp. 1–12.

Kohli, R., Arteaga, N., and McGovern, E. R. (2019). "Compliments" and "Jokes": Unpacking Racial Microaggressions in the K-12 Classroom. In: G. C. Torino, D. P. Rivera, C. M. Capodilupo, K. L. Nadal, & D. W. Sue, eds, *Microaggression Theory: Influence and Implications*. Hoboken, NJ: Cam Wiley & Sons, pp. 267–290.

Kwon, S. A. (2008). Moving From Complaints to Action: Oppositional Consciousness and Collective Action in a Political Community. *Anthropology & Education Quarterly*, 39(1), pp. 59–76.

Labrador, R. N. and Wright, E. K. (2011). Engaging Indigeneity in Pacific Islander and Asian American Studies. *Amerasia Journal*, 37(3), pp. 135–147.

Ladson-Billings, G. and Tate, W.F.I.V. (1995). Toward a Critical Race Theory of Education. *Teachers College Record*, 97(1), pp. 47–68.

Ladson-Billings, G. (2006). From the Achievement Gap to the Education Debt: Understanding Achievement in U.S. schools. *Educational Researcher*, 35(7), p. 3–10.

Leaders of a Beautiful Struggle (2014). Do Articles About 'Alternative Debate' Reinforce White Supremacy? Retrieved from: https://lbsbaltimore.com/do-articles-about-alternative-debate-reinforce-white-supremacy/ Retrieved on Oct 4, 2022, from: to share with the school, local libraries, and other spaces

Lee, S. (2009). *Unraveling the 'Model Minority' Stereotype: Listening to Asian American Youth*. New York, NY: Teachers College Press.

Leonardo, Z. (2009). *Race, Whiteness, and Education*. New York, NY: Routledge.

Leonardo, Z. (2012). The Race for Class: Reflections on a Critical Raceclass Theory of Education. *Education Studies*, 48, pp. 427–449.

Leonardo, Z. and Broderick, A. A. (2011). Smartness as Property: A Critical Exploration of the Intersections Between Whiteness and Disability Studies. *Teachers College Record*, 113(10), pp. 2206–2232.

Lewis, A. and Diamond, J. B. (2015). *Despite the Best Intentions: How Racial Inequality Thrives in Good Schools*. New York, NY: Oxford University Press.

Libassi, C. J. (2018). The Neglected College Race Gap: Racial Disparities Among College Completers. Retrieved from American Progress Institute.

Lipman, P. (2011). *The New Political Economy of Urban Education*. New York, NY: Routledge.

Love, B. (2019). *We Want to do More Than Survive: Abolitionist Teaching and the Pursuit of Educational Freedom*. Boston: Beacon Press Books.

Madkins, T.C. (2011). The Black Teacher Shortage: A Literature Review of Historical and Contemporary Trends. *The Journal of Negro Education*, 80(3), pp. 417–427.

Mangual Figueroa, A. (2011). Citizenship and Education in the Homework Completion Routine. *Anthropology & Education Quarterly*, 42(3), pp. 263–280.

Marucci, O. (2017). Zora Neal Hurston and the Brown Debate: Race, Class, and the Progressive Empire. *The Journal of Negro Education*, 86(1), 13–24.

Massey, D. S., and Denton, N. A. (1993). *American Apartheid: Segregation and the Making of the Underclass*. Cambridge, MA: Harvard University Press.

McGinley, A. C. (2019). The Masculinity Mandate: #MeToo, Brett Kavanaugh, and Christine Blasey Ford., *23 Employment Rights & Employment Policy Journal*, 59, pp. 59–83.

McKinney de Royston, M. (2020). Black Womanist Teachers' Political Clarity in Theory and Practice. *Theory Into Practice*, 59(4), pp. 379–388.

Maher, K. H. (2004). Borders and Social Distinction in the Global Suburb. *American Quarterly*, 56(3), pp. 781–806.

Meiners, E. (2016). *For the Children?: Protecting Innocence in a Carceral State*. Minneapolis, MN: University of Minnesota Press.

Mitchell, T. D., Donahue, D. M., and Young-Law, C. (2012). Service Learning as a Pedagogy of Whiteness. *Equity & Excellence in Education*, 45(4), pp. 612–929.

Moll, L. C. and Amanti, C. (1992). Funds of Knowledge for Teaching: Using a Qualitative Approach to Connect Homes and Classrooms. *Theory into Practice*, 31(2), pp. 132–141.

Moraga, C. and Anzaldua, G. (1983). *This Bridge Called my Back: Writings by Radical Women of Color*. New York. NY: Kitchen Table Press.

Morrill, A. (2016). Time Traveling Dogs (And Other Native Feminist Ways to Defy Dislocations). *Cultural Studies/Critical Methodologies*, 17(1), pp. 14–20.

Morris, M. (2018). *Pushout: The Criminalization of Black Girls in Schools*. New York, NY: New Press.

Nakano Glenn, E. (1992). From Servitude to Service Work: Historical Continuities in the Racial Division of Paid Reproductive Labor. *Journal of Women in Culture and Society*, 18(1), pp. 1–43.

Nasser, L. (2022). Debatable. Radiolab. NPR. Retrieved October 4, 2022 from radiolab.org/episodes/debatable-2205.

National Center for Education Statistics (September 2020). Race and Ethnicity of Public School Teachers and their Students. U.S. Department of Education. https://nces.ed.gov/pubs2020/2020103/index.asp

Nespor, J. (1997). *Tangled Up in School: Politics, Space, Bodies, and Signs in the Educational Process*. Mahwah, NJ: Lawrence Erlbaum Associates.

Oakes, J. (2005). *Keeping Track: How Schools Structure Inequality*. 2nd ed. New Haven, CT: Yale University Press.

Ogbar, J. O. G. (2019). *Black Power: Radical Politics and African American Identity*. Baltimore, MD: Cams Hopkins University Press.

Oliver, M. L. and Shapiro, T. M. (2006). *Black Wealth, White Wealth: A New Perspective on Racial Inequality*. 10th anniversary ed. New York, NY: Routledge.

Oliver, M. L., and Shapiro, T. M. (2008). Sub-Prime as a Black Catastrophe. *The American Prospect*, 19(10). Available at: http://prospect.org/article/sub-prime-black-catastrophe.

Osanloo, A. F., Boske, C., and Newcomb, W. S. (2016). Deconstructing Macroaggressions, Microaggressions, and Structural Racism in Education: Developing a Conceptual Model for the Intersection of Social Justice Practice and Intercultural Education. *International Journal of Organizational Theory and Development*, 4(1), pp. 1–18.

Paperson, L. (2010). The Postcolonial Ghetto: Seeing her Shape in his Hand. *Berkeley Review of Education*, 1(1), 5–34.

Patel, L. (2013). *Youth Held at the Border: Immigration, Education, and the Politics of Inclusion*. New York, NY: Teachers College Press.

Patel, L. (2016). *Decolonizing Education: From Ownership to Answerability*. New York, NY: Routledge.

Patillo, M. (2013). *Black Picket Fences: Privilege and Peril Among the Black Middle Class*. Chicago, IL: The University of Chicago Press.

Perry, P. (2002). *Shades of White: White Kids and Racial Identities in High School*. Durham, NC: Duke University Press.

Pollock, M. (2004). *Colormute: Race Talk Dilemmas in an American High School*. Princeton, NJ: Princeton University Press.

Posey, L. (2014). *When Middle-Class Parents Choose Urban Schools: Class, Race, and the Challenge of Equity in Public Education*. Chicago, IL: University of Chicago Press.

Quijano, A. (2000). Coloniality of Power, Eurocentrism, and Latin America. *Nepantla: Views from the South*, 1(3), pp. 533–580.

Quinn, T. and Meiners, E. (2009). *Flaunt It! Queers Organizing for Public Education and Justice*. New York, NY: Peter Lang.

Reddy-Best, K. L. (2019). "Male Hair Cannot Extend Below Plane of the Shoulder" and "No Cross Dressing": Critical Queer Analysis of High School Dress Codes in the United States. *Journal of Homosexuality*, 67, pp., 1290–1340.

Rickford, R. (2016). *We are an African People: Independent Education, Black Power, and the Radical Imagination*. New York, NY: Oxford University Press.

Rios, V. (2012). *Punished: Policing the Lives of Black and Latino Boys*. New York, NY: New York University Press.

Robinson, C. J. (2019). *Cedric J. Robinson: On Racial Capitalism, Black Internationalism, and Cultures of Resistance*, T. L. T. Quan. Ed. London, UK: Pluto Press.

Roediger, D. (2007). *The Wages of Whiteness: Race and the Making of the American Working Class*. New York: Verso.

Rosales, A. (1997). *Chicano! The History of the Mexican Civil Rights Movement*. 2nd Ed. Houston, TX: Arte Público Press.

Rothstein, R. (2017). *The Color of Law: A Forgotten History of how our Government Segregated America*. New York, NY: Liveright Publishing Corporation.

Self, R. O. (2003). *American Babylon: Race and the Struggle for Postwar Oakland*. Princeton, NJ: Princeton University Press.

Siddle Walker, V. (1996). *Their Highest Potential: An African American School Community in the Segregated South*. Raleigh, NC: University of North Carolina Press.

Simmons, L. (2019). *The Prison School: Educational Inequality and School Discipline in the Age of Mass Incarceration*. Oakland, CA: University of California Press.

Smith, N. (1996). *The New Urban Frontier: Gentrification and the Revanchist City*. London, NY: Routledge.

Soung, P. (2011). Social and Biological Constructions of Youth: Implications for Juvenile Justice and Racial Equity. *Northwestern Journal of Law & Social Policy*, 6(2), pp. 428–444.

Stovall, D. (2018). Normalizing Black Death: Michael Brown, Marissa Alexander, Dred Scott, and the Apartheid State. In: K. Fasching-Varner and N.D. Hartlep, eds., *The Assault on Communities of Color: Exploring the Realities of Race-Based Violence*. Lanham, MD: Rowman & Littlefield, pp. 65–72.

Takaki, R. (1990). *A Different Mirror: A History of Multicultural America*. Revised Edition. New York, NY: Back Bay Books.

Takaki, R. (2008). *Strangers From a Different Shore: A History of Asian Americans*. New York, NY: Penguin.

Tatum, B. D. (2017). *Why are all the Black Kids Sitting Together in the Cafeteria? And Other Observations About Race*. New York, NY: Basic Books.

Tillman, L. C. (2004). (Un)intended Consequences?: The Impact of the Brown v. Board of Education Decision on the Employment Status of Black Educators. *Education and Urban Society*, 36(3), pp. 208–303.

Torino, G. C., Rivera, D. P., Capodilupo, C. M., Nadal, K. L. & Sue, D. W., eds. (2019). *Microaggression Theory: Influence and Implications*. Hoboken, NJ: Cam Wiley & Sons, pp. 267–290.

Torres, L. (2018). Latinx? *Latino Studies*, 16, pp. 283–285.

Tuck, E. (2009). Suspending Damage: A Letter to Communities. *Harvard Educational Review*, 79(3), pp. 409–427.

Tuck, E. and Yang, W. K. (2012). Decolonization is Not a Metaphor. *Decolonization, Indigeneity, Education & Society*, 1(1), pp. 1–40.

Valenzuela, A. (1999). *Subtractive Schooling: U.S.-Mexican Youth and the Politics of Caring*. New York, NY: State University of New York Press.

Villegas, F. J. and Villegas, P. E. (2019). Bordered Lives: An Autoethnography of Transnational Precarity. In: E. Hurd, ed., *The Reflexivity of Pain and Privilege: Auto-Ethnographic Collections of Mixed Identity*. Boston: Brill Sense, pp. 175–190.

Villenas, S. (1996). The Colonizer/Colonized Chicana Ethnographer: Identity, Marginalization, and Co-optation in the Field. *Harvard Educational Review*, 66(4), pp. 711–731.

Walker, V. S. (1996). *Their Highest Potential: An African American School Community in the Segregated South*. Durham, NC: University of North Carolina Press.

Waitoller, F. (2020). *Excluded by Choice: Urban Students with Disabilities in the Education Marketplace*. New York, NY: Teachers College Press.

Weinberg, M. (2009). *Asian American Education: Historical Background and Current Realities*. New York, NY: Routledge

Willinsky, J. (1998). *Learning to Divide the World: Education at Empire's End*. Minneapolis, MN: University of Minnesota Press.

Wun, C. (2014). Unaccounted Roundations: Black Girls, Anti-Black Racism, and Punishment in Schools. *Critical Sociology*, 42(4-5), pp.737–750.

Yonezawa, S., Wells, A. S., and Serena, I. (2002). Choosing Tracks: "Freedom of Choice" in Detracking Schools, *American Educational Research Journal*, 39(1), pp. 37–67.

Yosso, T. (2006). *Critical Race Counterstories Along the Chicana/Chicano Educational Pipeline*. New York: Routledge.

Zimmer, R., Buddin, R., Smith, S. A., and Duffy, D. (2019). Nearly Three Decades into the Charter School Movement what has Research told us About Charter Schools? (EdWorkingPaper No. 19-156). Retrieved from Annenberg Institute at Brown University: http://www.edworkingpapers.com/ai, pp. 19–159.

Recommended projects, assignments, and discussion questions

1) Investigate your own community's histories of displacement and dispossession. Choose a place you grew up or have lived or studied in the past or currently. Please note that if you live in an all or almost all white space in the US, this space has been made this way, whether through Indigenous displacement, racially exclusionary laws and practice, or some combination of these, so this question is still relevant to you. If you live/d outside of the United States, white supremacy may be operative, but other significant social and political divisions may also shape educational inequalities, segregations, and dispossessions. You may address these if that's what feels right for this assignment. Try to learn.

   a. Whose Indigenous land are/were you on? Use this link: https://native-land.ca/
   b. In what ways have people been displaced to or from this land over time?

    c. How was this displacement, dispossession, or (de)segregation taught to and understood by you growing up (or more recently)?
    d. Reflecting on this context, which and whose knowledges are valued in the schools you grew up in or those in your communities and how?
    e. Where were/are other knowledges constructed, sustained, remembered, celebrated, and valued?

2) Memo, Khalil, and Elijah all engaged in theorization of, education about, and resistance to the social and educational circumstances they were facing through music. Music has a long history of serving as a space of knowledge production, particularly for people systematically excluded from and oppressed within schools. For this assignment, find a song that contains an analysis or critique of schooling embedded within it. Maybe even create and curate a playlist. Ask yourself:

    a. In what ways do you see (de)segregation, displacement, and dispossession in this song? Give examples of each if possible.
    b. What strategies for countering these do you see evident in the music, lyrics, context, or analysis?
    c. How is this song connected to movements, organizing, action, events, and circumstances that were happening on the ground? Who besides the author was involved in creating and spreading this music?
    d. In what ways does the music function as a space of learning, theorization, and knowledge production? For you and for others?

3) A lot of people think of segregation as just being about separation or exclusion. In this way, it's easy to think that coming together, erasing or ignoring difference, or opening up exclusive spaces is a solution. For this project, trace out some of the roots of and relationships between different ways of struggling for justice in the face of structural displacement, occupation, violence, and dispossession in and beyond education. In particular, do some research on Black-, Indigenous-, and people-of-color-led movements, projects, and theories in education that looked towards two or more of these different aims—integration, sovereignty, justice, celebration, self-knowledge, dignity, or assimilation. Ask yourself:

   a. What are some of the debates people were having over goals and strategies?
   b. How were these shaped by and in response to broader structures of power?
   c. How did these movements re-create education? How did they re-construct or re-imagine the future and the past?

Suggested further reading

Chapter 1: Memo

Abrego, L. J. (2014). *Sacrificing Families: Navigating Laws, Labor, and Love Across Borders*. Stanford, CA: Stanford University Press.

Abrego's qualitative work with separated families in El Salvador and the US looks at the myriad sacrifices families make in the quest for social and economic security and the ways families are sacrificed by governments. The text highlights the toll family separation takes on children and how migration's rewards are inequitably distributed by gender, class, and documentation status.

Mangual Figueroa, A. (2011). Citizenship and Education in the Homework Completion Routine. *Anthropology & Education Quarterly*, 42(3), pp. 263–280.

This is one of a series of articles by Mangual Figueroa that looks at how mixed status families (families where some members are undocumented) navigate everyday schooling routines and decisions.

Patel, L. (2013). *Youth Held at the Border: Immigration, Education, and the Politics of Inclusion*. New York, NY: Teachers College Press.

Patel addresses the myriad borders young people face as they navigate educational barriers, shifting documentation statuses and race, gender, class and other layers of identity.

Valenzuela, A. (1999). *Subtractive Schooling: U.S.-Mexican Youth and the Politics of Caring*. New York, NY: State University of New York Press.

This vivid ethnography offers insight into how schools subtract cultural resources and social networks from young people through assimilationist and aesthetic policies and practices.

Chapter 2: Jaqueline

Smith, N. (1996). *The New Urban Frontier: Gentrification and the Revanchist City*. London, NY: Routledge.

Smith's account of gentrification in New York looks not just at the politics and practices that shape gentrification, but also at the cultural politics of it. His understanding of how logics of the frontier pervade the occupation of urban space powerfully shaped my thinking.

Lipman, P. (2011). *The new political economy of urban education*. New York, NY: Routledge.

Lipman's text looks at how urban policy has shaped mass displacement, school closure and privatization. She looks at the right to the city as a framework for resisting these practices.

Beauboeuf-Latontant, T. (2002). A Womanist Experience of Caring: Understanding the Pedagogy of Exemplary Black Women Teachers. *The Urban Review: Issues and Ideas in Public Education*, 35(1), pp. 71-86.

Beauboeuf-Lafontant looks at the political, social, and pedagogical practices of Black womanist teachers. This article is important for thinking about what it means to be "with us" pedagogically.

hooks, B. (1997). *Yearning: Race, Gender, and Cultural Politics*. Boston, MA: South End Press.

This is one among many of hooks' powerful texts in which she elaborates on teaching, community, love, feminism, and anti-oppressive work. In this book she first theorizes "homeplace" and reflects on the organizing practices, strategies and labor of Black women and women of color.

Chapter 3: Cam

Leonardo, Z. (2009). *Race, Whiteness, and Education*. New York, NY: Routledge.

Leonardo's text is a vital resource in understanding how whiteness is produced in and through schools. It offers a thorough conceptual primer on whiteness and critical approaches to pedagogy and schools.

Hagerman, M. A. (2018). *White Kids: Growing Up With Privilege in a Racially Divided America*. New York, NY: New York University Press.

Hagerman addresses everyday ways whiteness is reproduced in families and communities and the ways white kids work with and rework these understandings.

Meiners, E. (2016). *For the Children?: Protecting Innocence in a Carceral State*. Minneapolis, MN: University of Minnesota Press.

Meiners looks at how ideas about whiteness, childhood, and innocence shape the carceral state. They work to understand how the criminalization and mass incarceration of young people of color is tied to the constructed, imagined, and protected innocence of white children.

Nakano Glenn, E. (1992). From Servitude to Service Work: Historical Continuities in the Racial Division of Paid Reproductive Labor. *Journal of Women in Culture and Society*, 18(1), pp. 1-43.

Nakano Glenn's text addresses how care chains function and their effects on migrant women and families. She traces the care labor of migrant women across borders and looks at how understandings of caring shape exploitive structures.

Chapter 4: Amy

Applebaum, B. (2010). Being White, Being Good: White Complicity, White Moral Responsibility, and Social Justice Pedagogy. Lanham, MD: Lexington Books.

Applebaum's text is important for thinking about the relationship between whiteness and goodness and how well intentioned and seemingly antiracist white action can be complicit in racial injustice.

Perry, P. (2002). Shades of white: White kids and racial identities in high school. Durham, NC: Duke University Press.

Perry addresses different manifestations of whiteness in different educational contexts, accounting for intersections of class, space, school, and school structure.

Kēhaulani, N. B. (2022). Tender Violence in US Schools: Benevolent Whiteness and the Dangers of Heroic White Womanhood. New York, NY: Routledge.

Kēhaulani offers a powerful critique of seemingly benevolent whiteness and the construct of white womanhood vis a vis the colonial state.

Danns, D. (2020). Crossing Segregated Boundaries: Remembering Chicago School Desegregation. Rutgers University Press.

Danns looks at the history of school desegregation in Chicago and argues that, when actually enacted, school desegregation had powerful impacts on the racial consciousness of students who participated, creating transformative change.

Chapter 5: Khalil

Paperson, La (2010). The postcolonial ghetto: Seeing her shape in his hand. *Berkeley Review of Education*, *1*(1), 5-34.

Through the lens of his and his students experience with school creation and closure, La Paperson engages with how education and ghettoized spaces are imagined, navigated, appropriated, and contested in debates about urban space, youth, and educational policy.

Hill, J. H. (2008). *The Everyday Language of White Racism*. Malden, MA: Wiley-Blackwell.

Hill looks from the perspective of a linguistic-anthropologist at how racial hierarchies are re-enacted through white racial discourse and practices including linguistic appropriation and discrimination.

Oliver, M. L. and Shapiro, T. M. (2006). *Black wealth, White wealth: A New Perspective on Racial Inequality*. 10th anniversary ed. New York, NY: Routledge.

Oliver and Shapiro look in detail at wealth as a tool for measuring and understanding the reproduction of racial inequality.

Chapter 6: Talli

Fullilove, M. T. (2004). *Root Shock: How Tearing up City Neighborhoods Hurts America and What We Can Do About It*. New York, NY: Random House.

Fullilove's book addresses histories of Black displacement and the impact on community and individual health of "urban renewal."

Love, B. (2019). *We Want to do More Than Survive: Abolitionist Teaching and the Pursuit of Educational Freedom*. Boston: Beacon Press Books.

This text offers a powerful critique of the interrelationship between structural and educational violence. Focusing on Black and Brown communities, Love argues towards and gives examples of abolitionist teaching that defies criminalizing and deficit logics.

Siddle Walker, V. (1996). *Their Highest Potential: An African American School Community in the Segregated South*. Raleigh, NC: University of North Carolina Press.

Siddle Walker tells the story of high expectations at a segregated Black school in North Carolina. She argues that the way we tell the story of desegregation erases the educational work, value, and life of Black educational spaces and practice.

Chapter 7: Rahul

Ferguson, A. A. (1995). *Bad Boys: Public Schools in the Making of Black Masculinity*. Ann Arbor, MI: University of Michigan Press.

This is a somewhat older text but really important for understanding how masculinities are produced through school practices.

Camacho, K. (2021). Reppin': Pacific Islander Youth and Native Justice. Seattle, WA: University of Howard Press.

This compilation of essays looks at Pacific Islander youth experiences, identity, and practices from a variety of perspectives and locations. It focuses, in particular, on resistance to criminalization, colonization, incarceration, and militarization.

Lewis, A. and Diamond, J. B. (2015). *Despite the Best Intentions: How Racial Inequality Thrives in Good Schools*. New York, NY: Oxford University Press.

This book looks at basic practices such as opportunity hoarding, disciplinary inequality, and tracking shape racial inequality in "good schools".

Fabricant, M. & Fine, M. (2013). The Changing Politics of Education: Privatization and the Dispossessed Lives Left Behind. Boulder: Paradigm Publishers.

Fabricant and Fine use political economic analysis to explore multiple, layered forms and sites of dispossession, situating these in the context of racist and neoliberal policymaking and practice.

Chapter 8: Jonathan

Weinberg, M. (2009). *Asian American Education: Historical Background and Current Realities*. New York, NY: Routledge

Weinberg describes the diversity of Asian-American educational histories and experiences. He looks at different national histories both in Asian countries and in the U.S. taking account of diversity within groups, change over time, and responses to discriminatory policy and practice.

Lee, S. (2009). *Unraveling the 'Model Minority' Stereotype: Listening to Asian American Youth*. New York, NY: Teachers College Press.

Lee offers vital tools for understanding how Asian and Asian-American students navigate their identities in K-12 schools and how the model minority stereotype can harm them and others.

Takaki, R. (2008). *Strangers From a Different Shore: A History of Asian Americans*. New York, NY: Penguin.

Takaki's text details the complexities of Asian-American experiences in the United States and the policies and practices that have shaped these.

Chapter 9: Elijah

Ewing, E. (2020). *Ghosts in the Schoolyard: Racism and School Closings on Chicago's South Side*. Chicago, IL: University of Chicago Press.

Ewing offers a searing account of how school closure and the disregard of the powerful work done in Black and Brown schools labeled as "bad" affect communities and children.

Rickford, R. (2016). *We are an African People: Independent Education, Black Power, and the Radical Imagination*. New York, NY: Oxford University Press.

Rickford documents the creative independent educational movements in different Black communities as these intersected with different social and political movements and theoretical approaches to inequality.

Desmond, M. (2016). *Evicted: Poverty and Profit in the American City*. New York: Broadway Books.

Desmond highlights the structural forces producing housing instability and insecurity and the excruciating experiences of people and families faced with eviction.

Index

(de)segregation. 20, 21, 71, 135, 216; desegregation. 8, 9, 21, 35, 45, 54, 60, 61, 113, 114, 122, 147, 168, 196, 197; integration. 32, 197, 198, 215

ableism. 87

African American. 13, 17, 24, 61, 108, 140, 180

antiblackness. 16

arts. 68, 118, 184, 193, 200, 201, 204

Asian. 18, 19, 31, 76, 79, 80, 97, 162, 178, 182, 183, 184, 185, 186, 208, 220, 223, 238, 239

Asian-American. 18

at risk. 77

bilingual. 45, 46, 54, 219

BIPOC. 15, 214, 221

Black. 15, 16, 18, 19, 23, 31, 33, 40, 41, 42, 45, 53, 54, 58, 59, 60, 66, 68, 79, 80, 87, 88, 91, 118, 126, 129, 134, 137, 138, 139, 143, 145, 146, 152, 158, 166, 171, 173, 174, 180, 187, 191, 192, 194, 196, 198, 202, 207, 208, 214, 215, 218, 219, 220, 222, 224, 225, 227, 234, 237, 238

Black and Brown. 16, 19, 21, 59, 60, 88, 143, 146, 194, 222

Black Language. 180

Black Lives Matter.

blockbusting. 59

borders. 23, 34, 45, 71, 72, 73

capitalism. 15, 221

charter schools. 149

coloniality. 15, 103; colonization. 50

colorblind. 23, 95, 135, 144, 198

colorblind racism. 23

colormute. 95

community. 121

community college. 48, 70, 131, 133, 151, 166, 175

course selection; tracking. 123

damage. 23, 36, 208

Deferred Action for Childhood Arrivals. 49

deficit. 35, 36, 50; *deficit narrative*. 35

deportation. 43

desegregation. 148

displacement. 15, 18, 20, 28, 29, 33, 34, 38, 58, 61, 62, 63, 71, 72, 117, 135, 156, 206, 207, 208, 215, 216

dispossession. 20, 23, 33, 63, 71, 135, 137, 142, 147, 155, 156, 211, 212, 214, 215, 216, 220; accumulation by dispossession. 155

Donald Trump. 135

dress code. 89

English-only. 46

eviction. 207, 208

frontier. 20, 23, 71, 72, 214

funds of knowledge. 33

gentrification. 27, 58, 63, 155, 207, 214, 234

ghettoization. 50

global care chains. 83

globalization. 32, 33, 34

homeplace. 28

hyper-surveillance. 146, 170

identity. 18, 20, 49, 162, 165, 166

Immigration and Customs Enforcement. 38

Indian Fijian. 163

Indigenous. 15, 18, 19, 51, 71, 103, 137, 214, 215

injustice. 14, 35, 39, 50, 64, 184, 201, 216

interest convergence. 197

invisibility. 82

invisibilization. 170

joy. 148, 164, 190, 192, 193, 207, 216

Korean. 138

labor. 28, 35, 83, 84, 98, 109, 131, 142, 152, 156, 190, 207

Language advocacy. 46

language justice. 44

language policy. 46

Latina. 54

Latino. 4, 17, 34, 57, 108, 227

Latinx. 16, 17, 19, 23, 31, 44, 45, 47, 54, 60, 80, 158, 166, 174, 181, 191, 192, 208

learning objectives. 20

Limited English Proficient. 25

low-income. 69

Mexican-American. 44

microaggressions. 124, 184; microassaults. 124

Military recruiting. 131

multicultural curriculum. 101

music. 201

myth of meritocracy. 99

opportunity gaps. 33

Pacific Islander. 18, 19, 31, 80, 138, 162, 163, 166, 174, 192, 208, 219, 220, 223, 238

parents. 1, 6, 8, 13, 21, 25, 31, 32, 36, 37, 51, 53, 56, 57, 60, 62, 64, 70, 79, 83, 84, 86, 88, 90, 91, 98, 105, 109, 138, 142, 143, 148, 165, 178, 183, 184, 196, 204

people of color. 15, 20, 54, 137, 145, 171, 173, 206

place. 28; place-making. 28

play Indian. 103

police brutality. 172

police harassment. 132

Polynesian. 18, 164, 165, 191, 197; Indian Fijian. 24

Polynesians. 68

predatory equity. 27, 38, 116

privatized. 58

privilege. 15, 17, 27, 62, 84, 99, 102, 103, 111, 113, 145, 147, 190, 201, 213

Proposition 227. 46

pseudoscience of race. 100

public/private. 95

raceclass. 14, 20

racial covenants. 59

racial ignorance. 84

racial justice. 16, 46, 121, 212

racial solidarity. 15, 47

racial violence. 23, 42

racism. 19, 42, 53, 60, 70, 87, 125, 132, 135, 140, 144, 146, 147, 148, 160, 172, 184, 185, 198, 202, 207, 212

redlining. 59

resilience. 20, 35

resistance. 15, 20, 32, 45, 57, 61, 148, 198, 207, 216

resource hording. 212

return on investment. 131

Samoan. 51, 163, 167, 173, 187

school to confinement pipeline. 171

school to prison pipeline. 171

segregation. 20, 21, 29, 32, 41, 44, 47, 71, 113, 114, 144, 148, 160, 183, 184, 186, 197, 211

Serrano v. Priest. 60

Service-learning. 82

settler colonial. 16, 98

sexuality or gender identity. 150

social isolation. 130, 132, 134, 150

social networks. 130

socially constructed. 14, 18

South Asian. 158

spirit murder. 216

sub-prime. 26, 143, 226

subtractive schooling. 130

survivance. 163

suspension. 83, 149, 158, 164, 165, 167, 168, 170, 171, 175; suspension and expulsion. 169

technology. 5, 7, 119, 127, 129

the frontier. 71

Tongan. 13, 51, 138, 145, 147, 163, 164, 167, 187

tracking. 32; de-tracking. 57; high tracked kids.; lower-tracked. 35

trauma. 174

Treaty of Guadalupe Hidalgo. 18

undocumented. 31, 48

wealth. 19, 26, 59, 60, 78, 142, 143, 144, 151, 237

wealthy. 8, 19, 26, 32, 35, 57, 60, 78, 84, 88, 102, 141, 143, 209

white. 22, 32, 54, 60, 208; white middle-classness. 22

white flight. 23, 45, 60, 143, 148, 198

white kid's. 126

white kids. 13, 31, 39, 64, 67, 68, 69, 91, 125, 127, 133, 134, 145, 146, 197, 214

white people. 62

white savior. 23, 47; saviors. 36

white space; pure white spaces. 212, 215

whiteness. 15, 19, 22, 27, 40, 45, 54, 57, 71, 77, 78, 82, 88, 98, 111, 112, 124, 132, 144, 160, 166, 184, 189, 213, 219, 223, 224, 227, 235; benevolent whiteness. 72

white woman's burden. 72

www.ingramcontent.com/pod-product-compliance
Lightning Source LLC
Chambersburg PA
CBHW070759230426
43665CB00017B/2421